# TWELVE DREAMS OF ROME

## MARINA ENGEL

EXPLORING THE POSSIBLE CITY

Culicidae
Architectural Press

Madison | Lemgo | Berlin

Culicidae Architectural Press
an imprint of Culicidae Press®
PO Box 5069
Madison, WI 53705-5069
USA
culicidaepress.com
editor@culicidaepress.com
+1 (352) 215-7558

TWELVE DREAMS OF ROME: EXPLORING THE POSSIBLE CITY
2025 © Marina Engel

All rights reserved. No part of this work covered by the copyright hereon may be reproduced or used in any form or by any means—graphic, electronic, or mechanical, including photocopying, recording, taping, or information storage and retrieval systems—without written permission of the publisher. Neither the author nor the publisher make any representation, express or implied, with regard to the accuracy of the information contained in this book and cannot accept any legal responsibility or liability for any errors or omissions that may be made.

The contents of this book was previously published in Italian as *12 Sogni di Roma. Esplorando la Città del Possibile*, © Castelvecchi, an imprint of Lit Edizioni

ISBN: 978-1-68315-128-9

culicidaepress.bsky.social – facebook.com/culicidaepress
threads.net/culicidaepress – x.com/culicidaepress
instagram.com/culicidaepress

Our books may be purchased in bulk for promotional, educational, and/or business use. Please contact your local bookseller or the Culicidae Press Sales Department at +1-352-215-7558 or by email at sales@culicidaepress.com

Book layout and design © 2025 by polytekton

To Joseph

# Table of Contents

Map                                                    6-7
Preface by Francesco Careri                               9
Introduction                                             15

## Dreams 1                                              25
### Rome's Youth
    Pietro and Fabrizio/Quarticciolo Ribelle      27
    Valerio/Fondazione Piccolo America            37
    Tommy/Scomodo                                 47
    Laura/Donnexstrada                            57

## Dreams 2                                              67
### Culture and Sport
    Claudia/Cubo Libro                            69
    Sylvia/Angelo Mai Altrove                     79
    Luca/Post Ex                                  89
    Massimo/Calciosociale                         99

## Dreams 3                                             109
### Urban Landscapes
    Francesco/Termini tv and Mama Termini        111
    Gigliola/Libera Repubblica di San Lorenzo    121
    Alessandra/Forum Territoriale Parco delle
        Energie — Lago Ex SNIA               131
    Stefania/Ecomuseo Casilino                   141

| | |
|---|---|
| Acknowledgements | 151 |
| Appendix | 153 |
| Recommendations | 153 |
|     Quarticciolo Ribelle | 153 |
|     Fondazione Piccolo America | 154 |
|     Scomodo | 155 |
|     Donnexstrada | 156 |
|     Cubo Libro | 157 |
|     Angelo Mai Altove | 158 |
|     Post Ex | 159 |
|     Calciosociale | 160 |
|     Termini tv/Mama Termini | 161 |
|     Libera Repubblica di San Lorenzo | 162 |
|     Forum Territoriale Parco delle Energie — Lago Ex SNIA | 163 |
|     Ecomuseo Casilino | 164 |

DREAMS 1 – Rome's Youth
1. Quarticciolo Ribelle, Quarticciolo
2. Fondazione Piccolo America, Trastevere
3. Scomodo, Esquilino
4. Donnexstrada (no headquarters)

DREAMS 2 – Culture and Sport
5. Cubo Libro, Tor Bella Monaca
6. Angelo Mai Altrove, Celio
7. Post Ex, Centocelle
8. Calciosociale, Corviale

DREAMS 3 – Urban Landscapes
9. Termini tv and Mama Termini, Stazione Termini
10. Libera Repubblica di San Lorenzo, San Lorenzo
11. Forum Territoriale Parco delle Energie - Lago Ex-Snia, Pigneto-Prenestino
12. Ecomuseo Casilino, Tor Pignattara, Centocelle

Map Design by Luca Lamorgese

# Preface

*If you ask, 'Why is Thekla's construction taking such a long time?' the inhabitants continue hoisting sacks, lowering leaded strings, moving long brushes up and down, as they answer, 'So that its destruction cannot begin.' And if asked whether they fear that, once the scaffoldings are removed, the city may begin to crumble and fall to pieces, they add hastily, in a whisper, 'Not only the city.'*

Italo Calvino, *Invisible Cities*, 1972

Marina Engel's book is not about the *urbs* but about the *civitas* — the city made of people and not the one made of stone. It tells us about a city made of dreams, of real places where walls disappear, where streets are streams of encounters and relationships, and where public spaces are people who dream together. It is a city of citizens, that recall the rousing words of the Greek Nicias to the Athenian soldiers on the beach at Syracuse: "you are yourselves the town, wherever you choose to settle... it is men that make the city, not the walls and ships without them..." I found this quote from Thucydides in Joseph Rykwert's seminal book on Rome, *The Idea of a Town: The Anthropology of Urban Form in the Ancient World*, first published in 1962. A few pages later, Rykwert continues: "But the town is not really like a natural phenomenon. It is an artifact — an artifact of a curious kind, compounded of willed and random elements, imperfectly controlled. If it is related to physiology at all, it is more like a dream than anything else." Joseph Rykwert and Italo Calvino were bound by a friendship forged during the years when Joseph wandered through Rome, probing its stones to discover archaic rituals and the cosmic meanings of its magical foundation. Calvino spoke of the influence of the 'Idea of a Town,' on the city-ideas in his book *Invisible Cities*, in which he warns us that if the city of Thekla is not constantly built with dreams, it will crumble and fall apart. And not only the stone city would vanish, but above all everything else: its social bonds, and the crucial and intimate relationships between humans, animals, and gods. The cites of stone are born in dreams, in the interplay between the conscious and the unconscious, in rituals that connect the day to the starry night, the city to the sky. I talk about this because Joseph Rykwert was not only Calvino's friend but also Marina Engel's adoptive father, as Rome is her adoptive city, where she has lived for decades.

Marina Engel narrates the dreams that continue to build the Eternal City. Twelve dreams — we could call them twelve invisible cities. Invisible, because they tell us about a Rome that many Romans do not know nor even imagine possible. Romans are often distracted — sometimes more than tourists — and they are certainly lazier; not only do they fail to see what lies in front of them, often they are unable to appreciate those small changes brought about by the determination of their fellow citizens. Indeed, these dreams are told by a foreign woman, a curious woman, a psycho-geographer who seeks out urban dreams, relying partly on the advice of her daughters, partly on friends, and partly on social media — often the only source. She contacts her dreamers and meets them in cafés, on the street, on the doorstep of their associations, during the initiatives they have invented, launched and defended. What she gathers are twelve experiences of reclaiming the meaning of making a city — a self-made city as Carlo Cellamare called it in his introduction to the Italian edition.

They are fragments of the city that would not exist had we waited for politicians, public officials, urban planners or architects to conceive and produce them. The strength of these places and these projects lies in their self-determination, in those forces that navigate the boundary between legal and illegal in order to bypass labyrinthine bureaucracy, norms and regulations. These dreams have the power to generate new norms: they pave the way for those who follow, bringing forth new uses and models for everyone. Above all, they make possible what at first had seemed inconceivable. And I emphasize that these dreams are collective — there is never a lone dreamer because alone, one goes nowhere — there is always a group of people willing to dream together, to lose time, to take risks, to roll up their sleeves, and to work on improving a small piece of the world and play its part in a global movement composed of numerous molecular revolutions. They are like invisible Lilliputians who move and repair stones amid the ruins of the Eternal City. They fight the usual enemies: privatization, real estate speculation, bureaucratic inertia, incompetence, foot-dragging, indifference, fear and boredom. And they fight to build simple places: study rooms, public cinemas, libraries, theaters, neighbourhood gyms, collective studios, open-air museums, food supplies for the homeless and political and cultural journals. With their dreams, they construct stories that are able to change a city—eternally gazing at the past, waiting for the future, and unable to live in the present — and be, as Stalker said, referring to Giles Deleuze, "worthy of what happens"— acting as poets and singers of the current age, of an era they did not choose but in which they had to live and decided to transform. They do not wait for change, but come together, and through their dreams they reshape space and time, their lives and the lives of others. At the end of every encounter, Marina asks her guests to share one more dream. And each person's dream is to continue dreaming.

Francesco Careri, Co-founder of Stalker/Osservatorio Nomade, Professor of Urban Design and Architecture, Roma Tre University and author of *Walkscapes: walking as an aesthetic practice* (Culicidae Architectural Press, 2017)

*By confronting the politics of alienation with a politics of belonging, we rekindle our imagination and discover our power to act.*

George Monbiot, *Out of the Wreckage: A New Politics for an Age of Crisis, Verso*, London, 2017.

# Introduction

"Are you still in Rome?" I am sometimes greeted with that question when I am stopped on the street by an old friend or acquaintance in London, my birthplace. And I know that, in their English way, what they are really trying to ask is 'why are you still stuck over there when you could be here where it is all happening?' It is as if Rome is seen as a beautiful city to visit but a boring one to reside in. I am often left feeling a little unsure of how to respond. Nor do I fare much better when I travel up to Northern Italy. In Milan I have been asked: "But you come from London; how can you cope with the chaos? And the Romans, they are so rude!" I occasionally resort to replying with clichés: the capital's timeless beauty, the sunlight in the late afternoon, the languid summer nights, the slower pace of life, the informal manner of its denizens and their unique sense of humor. While all this is true — and there are also those who envy what they imagine to be the Roman lifestyle — I knew that there was another story to tell.

An Italian activist once said to me: "Rome is full of extraordinary people." At the time, I thought it was a rather sentimental remark. After all, the Italian capital has its share of criminals, thugs and thieves just like any other place. Yet, I understood what she meant, she was impressed by their ability to arrangiarsi, (to get by): to join together to find solutions to seemingly impossible problems. What is most striking about the city is what Romans themselves call 'a special energy', one that is generated by its inhabitants. "The alternative is to sit and wait for the world to get better on its own; but it is not getting better, it's getting much worse," says Pietro Vicari at Quarticciolo Ribelle.

"In the absence of institutional support, citizens can only improve their living conditions by coming together as a community," he continues. Across the city, thousands, if not, tens of thousands of citizens are doing just that: forming self-managed organizations to re-appropriate public spaces in which they can congregate and opposing speculation and privatization to create civic spaces. They help reanimate their neighborhoods, help secure accommodation for the homeless, assist those in need, protect and enhance the environment, provide opportunities for the young, and promote independent culture and sports activities that are accessible to everyone. Much of this 'energy' derives from a disenchantment with mainstream politics and a distrust of institutions that fail to defend their rights. These collectives are more concerned with engaging in politics with a small 'p', a practice defined by their daily actions. "Rome is a city that needs trust to prosper, and trust is created by the support of citizens, by community-led care of the territory, opening spaces and not closing them," writes Luca Mascini, Militant A of Assalti Frontali, the Roman rap band.

"When you are sixteen, you think you can change the world [...] but then you realize that it won't happen, so, meanwhile, you start trying to change your neighborhood," says Fabrizio Troya at Quarticciolo Ribelle. Tourists, attracted by Rome's five-star hotel boom, may take comfort in the enduring presence of its monuments but the majority of the Roman population live outside the historic center, many in neighborhoods where tourists rarely venture. They wake up every morning to contend with a chaotic, dirty and noisy city in which the state is increasingly absent. A city where some neighborhoods are deprived of basic services, and where living conditions are tough; a city grappling with a housing emergency, an escalating cost-of-living crisis, high levels of early school drop-out rates in poorer districts, precarious employment as well as youth unemployment — and endemic corruption. Such conditions are not all unique to Rome or Italy. Neither is the emotional response: anger at social injustice and at the widening inequalities in wealth and opportunity is rampant. "I have tried to transform it into something positive instead of something destructive," says Claudia Bernabucci, at Cubo Libro in Tor Bella Monaca. Tommy Salaroli, at Scomodo, describes his "feelings of loneliness" and "a need to be part of something." Loneliness, the bane of the contemporary city, what is today referred to as the 'loneliness epidemic' with its disastrous impact on physical and mental health, is symptomatic of the breakdown of community across the Western world. Not surprisingly, activism, particularly among the young — who are also faced with the impending threat of climate change — is on the rise across Europe. But perhaps what is special to Rome, is the wealth of citizen's collectives determined to combat liberalist ideology to offer an alternative and inclusive vision of the city: a city of the possible.

While Northern Europe and the US confront the devastating aftermath of social isolation during the Covid-19 pandemic and slowly rediscover the importance of community, and as politicians, policy makers, academics, and urbanists brandish 'community building' or 'community regeneration' as their slogans, they might well choose to head south — where the concept of community has not been entirely forgotten — and take a look at what is happening in the Italian capital. While neighborhood regeneration, developing urban green areas, reusing buildings, as opposed to building new constructions — to name just a few actions — have become the subject matter of an infinite number of newspaper articles and the themes of international conferences, Roman citizens have been joining together for decades to pursue those very strategies. "Actions speak louder than words, but not nearly as often," famously wrote the author Mark Twain. Foreigners and even the odd Italian may be unaware that there is a whole other city — arguably one that is more interesting — that they have yet to experience.

Carlo Cellamare, Professor of Urban Planning at La Sapienza University, and an authority on community-led urban regeneration, calls Rome a 'Città-fai-da-te' (a Do-it-yourself-city), which is also the title of his book in which he analyses the wide spectrum of self-managed organizations in the city. Cellamare describes housing squats as the "mother of many other experiences." Certainly, Rome hosts one of the largest numbers of squats in Europe, as inhabitants join together to combat a housing crisis in which market-rate prices are extortionate and public housing is in short supply—in February 2023, nearly seventeen thousand families were registered on the public housing waiting list. Meanwhile, the Laboratorio CIRCO — at the Roma Tre University architecture faculty — has calculated that some eleven thousand people occupy Rome's numerous abandoned buildings. Today, two of Rome's most famous squats, Metropoliz and Porto Fluviale Occupato, are about to be requalified to provide legal accommodation. At Porto Fluviale — in Ostiense in central Rome — a collective of fifty-six homeless families of thirteen nationalities have restored and now self-govern a formerly derelict military warehouse in order to supply accommodation and offer a range of socio-cultural services to the neighborhood. Metropoliz — a former salami factory in Tor Sapienza in east Rome — was the first squat to host Roma alongside other ethnic groups. It is also home to the MAAM — Museo dell'altro e dell'altrove di Metropoliz (Museum of the Other and the Elsewhere of Metropoliz) — a contemporary art museum, established by the anthropologist and curator Giorgio de Finis, along with the squatters.

A long tradition of grassroots collective action has encouraged some of the city's most dynamic and creative socio-cultural experiments, from the social centers of the 1980s and their proliferation in the 1990s to the boom of independent creative spaces in the 2000s, from the range of self-governed associations operating today to Rome's vibrant independent cultural scene — performance art and theater, music and Roman rap, artists collectives, a female cultural underground community, and street art and poetry. "A characteristic of Rome," says the artistic duo Industria Independente, "is how human relationships are valued." Even though at times, there are tensions within organizations, as in every family — and antagonism between them.

This book concentrates on twelve organizations, and it would take many pages just to list some of the others. Well-known examples include: Nonna Roma, a banco di mutuo soccorso (a mutual aid bank) that, among other services, collects and distributes food and essential items to people on the margins of society; Liberi Nantes, a sports association that promotes free sports activities for refugees and asylum seekers; Baobab Experience that provides assistance to immigrants who arrive in Italy as well as those in transit, the Associazione Genitori Scuola Di Donato, where parents have opened up a school after hours, to offer socio-cultural services to pupils and members of the Esquilino neighborhood's multi-ethnic community, and the young Roman affiliates of Ultima Generazione (Last Generation) who are risking their futures to save this planet. With the exception of Corviale, most of the associations listed here are based in east Rome, and this book is also intended as an introduction for visitors to the capital to explore some of the livelier parts of the city. "The south-east has always been fiery," comments Stefania Favorito at the Ecomuseo Casilino.

Many of these collectives began their activities by occupying and renovating abandoned spaces. Today they are nearly all legal entities. They are represented by Romans or adopted Romans of varying ages, professions and social backgrounds. They recount their stories, their motives, their fears and their dreams. The first section — DREAMS 1 — is dedicated to the young, the future of this city: young people narrate how they are revitalizing and destigmatizing their neighborhood; rebuilding hope for their contemporaries and persuading them to leave their computer screens at home and come together to watch a movie or read a printed journal; and empowering women and gender minorities. In DREAMS 2 citizens describe ways of helping regenerate poorer districts through culture — a library and community space, and sport — an inclusive way of playing football, as well as reanimating an independent artistic scene — an artist's collective and one of Rome's best known independent cultural centers. DREAMS 3 considers urban landscapes: activists explain how they are defending and revalorizing some of the territory in east Rome; opposing privatization, helping integrate immigrant populations into Italian society and strengthening collective identity.

Common to all organizations is the ambition to raise awareness and enable citizens to reclaim their rights. And however big the obstacles they face, however numerous the setbacks they encounter, however precarious the foundations on which they stand and whatever divisions may exist between them, they are all animated by people who not only dream but also engage in initiatives that bring hope in bleak times. People who demonstrate by their daily actions — and daily commitment — that an alternative vision of the city is possible. Maybe the next time someone stops me on the street in London and asks me if I am still in Rome, I will be able to explain, with pride, why I am, yes, still here.

# DREAMS 1

## Rome's Youth

From the left: Pietro Vicari, Fabrizio Troya
Photo by Flavia Rizzuto, 2024

# Pietro and Fabrizio/Quarticciolo Ribelle

On a summer day, Quarticciolo is a handsome neighborhood. The yellow facades of its housing units gleam in the late afternoon sunlight. Low-rise buildings open onto internal courtyards and gardens, arranged on a pedestrian-friendly grid pattern. A huge mural by the street artist Blu covers the front of the one tall (and forbidding) structure, the former Casa del Fascio (Ex Fascist Party headquarters). There is a village feel to this public housing complex; an atmosphere that is not always to be found in the massive post-war residential complexes in other districts.

The main square, Piazza del Quarticciolo, is taken over by a colorful boxing-ring, just beneath Blu's mural. It is Quarticciolo's annual *Festa della Borgata* (the Borgata Party), organized by the collective Quarticciolo Ribelle (Rebellious Quarticciolo*)*. Many hundreds of locals have turned out to support the neighborhood's teen-age boxers as they compete against other regional clubs. Small children, future boxers, spur on the home team, as do parents, grand-parents — entire families, all packed around the four sides of the ring.

People greet each other, exchanging hugs. Even though I am obviously an outsider — and a foreigner — I am welcomed by friendly smiles. An elderly man beckons me to indicate a vacant spot on a low wall with a good view of the game. Pietro Vicari, an activist at Quarticciolo Ribelle, has described the "magnetic and theatrical quality" of a boxing match. Even I, who am clueless about boxing rules, feel hypnotized by the spectacle, intoxicated by the charged atmosphere. The crowd proudly cheers on young Flavio, dressed in fiery red. He seems to dance around his opponent. His athletic coaches, in green attire, Manu Agati and Fabrizio Troya, are on the side, waiting for the intermission signal, ready to leap onto the ring to encourage him. Everyone roars with delight when Flavio is later announced the winner, and they kindly applaud his defeated competitor.

Quarticciolo was designed by the architect Roberto Nicolini, during the fascist regime. The bulk of the buildings were constructed between 1938 and 1943, to accommodate a working-class population that was forcibly moved from the historic center to the *borgate* (working-class suburbs) in the city's outskirts, to make way for Mussolini's grandiose public works. When Allied bombing made residents homeless in neighborhoods nearby, they came to Quarticciolo to occupy buildings that were not yet completed. Descendants of some of those families continue to live in the original ten housing units — a total of two thousand four hundred flats that are managed by ATER (Rome's public-housing authority). Despite some renovations in the 1950s, buildings were poorly constructed and lacked basic services.

Arriving by public transport can be challenging. When I return to see Pietro and Fabrizio, the journey — down the via Prenestina on the number 14 tram from Termini (the main train station) — can take well over an hour. By car, it is a twenty-minute ride. A tour of the borgata with Pietro reveals numerous housing units in a state of decay. Water infiltration is widespread, he tells me, and some residents have to contend with toxic mold inside their homes. Extended families are frequently crammed into tiny lodgings. Others cope with makeshift accommodations assembled in the buildings' damp basements. Living conditions can be tough, particularly in a degraded area that locals have nicknamed the 'favelas'.

Pietro has an open face and a boyish smile but conveys a serious air beyond his thirty-three years. He walks fast and speaks even faster. He is not someone who has time to spare; he devotes his life to activism. To support himself, he works from Monday to Friday as a researcher on urbanism at a *centro studi* (study center). Early mornings, evenings and weekends are dedicated to his activities in the community. I have no idea how he found the time to finish a PhD on urbanism at Roma Tre University. "My girlfriend isn't always so happy about this," he says laughingly.

Pietro and his childhood friend Manu (Emanuele) turned to activism when they were teenagers in Rome. They have never looked back. In 2015, they decided to move to the poorer district of Quarticciolo. Impressed by the *palestre* (gyms) Manu visited in the Brazilian favelas while he trained to be a boxer, their objective was to found

Quarticciolo's own Palestra: an indoor space that offers sports activities to those who cannot afford them, and also serves as a community center. Along with local activists, including the then seventeen-year-old Fabrizio, they occupied a disused boiler house, restoring it themselves, with funds raised by residents. Soon, they were able to open the Palestra Popolare Quarticciolo — the only gym in the neighborhood — run by their collective called Quarticciolo Ribelle (Rebellious Quarticciolo).

We join Fabrizio at Rosi's bar at the Teatro Biblioteca Quarticciolo. "Pietro coordinates everyone — he is everywhere," says Fabrizio admiringly. "He understands the dynamics of any situation, and he can talk to anyone." "It would have been impossible to set up the Palestra without Fabrizio, Fiamma and other local residents," replies Pietro. Twenty-four-year-old Fabrizio has known everyone in the district since he was a child. Recently graduated, with a degree in physical education and sports science, Fabrizio has the self-assured ease of someone who is settled in his surroundings. Here, he is known as the grandson of Rosa Meffe, an activist leader in the fight for public housing. Generations of Meffes have lived in Quarticciolo. "It is like a village," says Fabrizio, "many families are inter-married." Family and social ties have forged a close-knit community that feels isolated from the rest of the city and abandoned by public authorities. It is also a "closed community that can exclude people," says Pietro. "Living here can be tiring," adds Fabrizio.

"Our work is to construct new forms of social ties," Pietro continues. "Boxing allows us to interact with people in an unobtrusive way." It is an activity that requires self-discipline and a healthy lifestyle. There are goals to be met for every match: training daily, sleeping regular hours and eating properly. By working on these targets with young people and their families, the collective acquired an understanding of living conditions; "when a family of six cohabit a thirty-five-square-meter space, they stop cooking," says Pietro. "In a neighborhood like this, having a Palestra with local boxers also gives a sense of security," says Fabrizio. Boxing has a long tradition in the Roman periphery. Above all, the Palestra provides young people with an alternative: Quarticciolo has one of the highest school drop-out rates in the city. The aim is to keep children in school and off the street. After-school support is on offer, as well as help with homework. Over the years, the Palestra has become a symbol of the borgata's pride. "It is like a protective cocoon," says Fabrizio. A popular meeting place for all generations, it has been instrumental in drawing the community together. Many local drug-dealers send their children to the Palestra. "They would prefer to see their child lead a different life," says Pietro.

Quarticciolo is one of Rome's four main drug-dealing centers, a subject that the media likes to exploit. "Maxi anti-drug raids are like military operations!" exclaims Pietro, "helicopters, closed roads, balaclavas, armed police enter homes breaking down doors. [...] I was shocked to see that six- and seven-year-old children (in the Palestra) were the ones who calmed us down; they were already used to it," he adds. When, on an early winter morning in 2017, residents were woken up by the sound of helicopters, they thought that they were witnessing another drug raid. Instead, Pietro told me, armed police had come to evict a family of five for constructing a papier mâché wall to divide a thirty square meter dwelling. One of the sons attended the Palestra.

Amid local outrage, Quarticciolo Ribelle set up the Comitato di Quartiere (Neighborhood Committee). Its first step was to prevent evictions and water-supply cuts. It then started work on a bigger operation: the improvement of living conditions. Their biggest victory, to date, has been to secure adequate housing for sixty families in the favelas, although it took long negotiations with ATER, as well as some demonstrations. There is a formidable battle ahead but Pietro, Fabrizio and their cohorts are driven by a sense of urgency. For Fabrizio, working at the Palestra is a way of engaging in politics; he has never voted and is disillusioned by mainstream parties. "The alternative is to sit and wait for the world to get better on its own, but it is not getting better, it is getting much worse," says Pietro. "When I look at other thirty-year-olds," he continues, they are "all experiencing a big crisis about the meaning of what they are doing […] often they are doing pointless work. But to find a consistency in the energy you spend and the impact you have, that is a real privilege."

Pietro and Manu came to Quarticciolo with what Pietro calls "a very classic idea about political intervention;" the focus was on "housing, education, access to sports activities." Community advocacy is now equally important: the need to empower residents and provide them with the tools to reclaim their rights. Pietro is determined to help change the public perception of Quarticciolo: to "destigmatize the borgata" and prevent residents being treated as "second-class citizens." They are used to feeling judged, he tells me. "Every time someone from Quarticciolo goes to any government office, he is in the wrong because he has made mistakes from the beginning: mistakes in the way he behaves, mistakes completing forms, mistakes in how he dresses, mistakes in how he communicates his problem [...] at school they ask him how he behaves with his children." The committee — Alessia, in particular — accompanies residents at every step, helping them navigate the labyrinths of Italian bureaucracy. "It is a pedagogical operation," he says, and they are beginning to see results.

When they started their activities, the majority of residents were ashamed of the borgata's stigma; they would go for a job interview and pretend they came from somewhere else. "Now they are quite proud of belonging to this community," says Pietro. "Their lives are different; they are no longer ashamed of where they come from." "But then you have to return to reality," replies Fabrizio, "you are not changing people's lives, you are just giving them a hand; their lives will only change when they have a different level of income, when you give them the opportunity to live the day rather than just survive it [...] you changed their lives when you moved the families out of the favelas." Pietro admits that the economic challenges remain "gigantic." It is a community of the working poor, he explains. By managing different jobs outside Quarticciolo, adults usually scrape together six hundred euros a month.

The collective has embarked on regenerating the neighborhood's economy but it will be hard to compete with drug-dealers who offer two thousand-euro monthly salaries to any teen-ager willing to act as a local sentinel. Nevertheless, there are plans to open a brewery, as well as a small printing house[1]. In the long run, local employment could stimulate commercial activities and bring life back to the neighborhood. "When you are sixteen, you think you can change the world […] but then you realize that it won't happen so, meanwhile, you start trying to change your neighborhood," says Fabrizio. After just eight years, about one member of every family regularly participates in Quarticciolo Ribelle's activities. Thousands attend their events. In 2021, a local crowdfunding campaign financed the adaptive reuse of an abandoned bowling green. The Palestra and the Comitato di Quartiere are now housed in one building: the *Casa di Quartiere* (Neighborhood House). A concessionary rent is paid to ATER. The after-school laboratory is nearby, and the former Palestra, in the process of being requalified by ATER, will host a doctor's office. "In the absence of institutional support, citizens can only improve their living conditions by coming together as a community," says Pietro. Quarticciolo Ribelle stands at the heart of that community, or the "family," as one elderly man proudly calls it.

---

[1] They opened in March 2024, together with the doctor's surgery.

The odds may still be high but perhaps Manu's dream of "creating a world, a society, more similar to the one he dreamed about," is not as far away as it might seem.[2]

---

[2] The far-right government in Italy is taking increasingly repressive measures and, as we go to print in 2025, the Ex Questura which provides accommodation for twenty families and hosts the after-school laboratory as well as the brewery, is under threat of eviction. Pietro is now working as a researcher in economic geography at Milan's Polytechnic.

From the left: Elèna Novelli, Agnese Rampini, Maria Sole Vulicevic, Vittoria Basile, Alice Catucci, Federico Croce, Valerio Carocci, Sara Pirone, Giulia Flor Buraschi, Letizia Yacoub, Oronzo Blonda, Nelson Papa, Dudu, Andrea Littera, Federico Rossi, Mario Dante, Gabriele Cocciarelli
Photo by Luca Dammicco, 2023

# Valerio/Fondazione Piccolo America

One autumn afternoon in 2012, my then fourteen-year-old daughter Gaia came running home, exhilarated by the discovery of a new venue in Trastevere — in central Rome — called Cinema America, an abandoned cinema that had been squatted and renovated by a collective of teenagers not much older than her. She and her friends had finally found a free study-room in the city — open all afternoon when high-schools are closed — where they could even see film classics for free! For decades I had walked past the cinema, a derelict building in the heart of one of the city's most enchanting neighborhoods, now overrun by tourists. So, curious to see the 'new cinema', I arranged to visit it with a friend. We arrived just in time to join a queue of young Romans, along with a sizable group of denizens our age, all waiting to see Rossellini's *Roma Città Aperta*, and managed to procure the last two seats as a large crowd of young teenagers rushed in and sat down on the floor in front of us.

With his considerable oratory skills, Valerio Carocci soon became the spokesman for the collective called the 'ragazzi del Cinema America' (boys and girls of the Cinema America). When I first met him some years ago, I was struck by his earnestness and boyish charm. Valerio is now a thirty-one-year-old adult; he has grown a short dark beard and is dressed entirely in black. While he has retained his pensive mien, he is more guarded. Like his companions, Valerio has had to grow up fast. "We are no longer the 'ragazzi del Cinema America'," he tells me right away, "we are the Fondazione Piccolo America." As the figurehead of the collective, Valerio has been scrutinized by the press from a young age and is weary of people coming to interview him. "Does it have to be me?" he asks. "I am nothing without the group […] for the last eleven years, the media, institutions and sponsors needed a recognizable face," he says; at the beginning, he lent his with enthusiasm but the collective's success has come at a "high human cost." It takes some persuasion to convince him. After hunting for a suitable location where we can conduct the interview, we end up sitting huddled together on an interior staircase, the only free space available at the Foundation's headquarters at the Cinema Troisi.

The collective was formed in 2012 by a group of students who were less interested in "participating in school and university political movements and more concerned with social action," says Valerio. Their focus was on the socio-economic divide between the city center and the urban periphery. Most of them lived in the suburbs and commuted daily by public transport to the center where they studied. The group needed a "muretto sotto casa," (local square) in the center, he says, a "safe place" where they could meet; a "study-room" and "home" in a privileged neighborhood that "should be accessible to everyone." Having unsuccessfully negotiated for a venue with the local government, they decided to map Rome's numerous abandoned buildings, of which forty were cinemas, including the Cinema America, designed by the architect Angelo di Castro in 1956. When, he tells me, in 2012, the building's owners received permission to demolish it to create a high-end apartment block, the collective joined the residents' protest, occupying the building to restore a cultural space to the community and to fight against continuing property speculation in the district. Local residents helped the youngsters raise enough funds to renovate the interior by themselves and establish a small library and study-room. At the time "no one (in the group) was a cinephile," says Valerio. But soon, they attracted an audience from across the city. A wealth of leading Italian cinema directors, including Nanni Moretti, Paolo Sorrentino and Carlo Verdone came to present their films and back the collective who eventually convinced the Beni Culturali (Ministry of Cultural Heritage) to list the building as being of historic interest and so prevent its demolition.

The police evicted the collective in 2014 but the momentum continued. The 'ragazzi' founded the Associazione Piccolo America as a legal non-profit organization and transferred temporarily to a local bakery that had been offered to them. In the summer of 2015, the association launched 'Il Cinema in Piazza' (Cinema in the Piazza) in the near-by piazza San Cosimato. Animated by a children's playground and market during the day; at night, the square was taken over by tourists and young people on drinking sprees in the near-by bars. With the help of the local municipality and the residents' association, the collective secured a giant screen, residents brought chairs, cushions and plates of pasta, and every evening, at sunset, for the following two months, local communities, children and grand parents alike, reappropriated the piazza and gathered to watch a film. Entrance was free. "They have done a splendid job and restored a real soul" to the neighborhood, says Piero Iacozzilli, who runs the grocery store inherited from his father between Cinema America and Piazza San Cosimato.

From thirty-six thousand spectators in 2015, to one hundred thousand over June and July 2023, "'Il Cinema in Piazza' has become Rome's biggest free event," says Valerio. Public and private sponsorship has multiplied — a budget of seven hundred thousand euros in 2023 — as has support from a range of international directors and actors including Oliver Stone, Wim Wenders, Richard Gere, and Jeremy Irons who have come to introduce their films and take part in debates with the public — not only in Trastevere but also in Rome's suburbs. Operating simultaneously at the Cervelletta in Colli Aniene, Valerio's home district in east Rome, and Monte Ciocci in west Rome,[3] Cinema in Piazza has united hundreds of thousands of citizens in front of the big screen and made cinema accessible to a segment of the general public that had never entered a cinema theater. Others have been inspired to venture to districts they had not visited previously. By erecting a cinema arena in the center of the degraded park,

---

[3] From 2018-2020, it operated in Ostia.

the Parco della Cervelletta — barely known to most Romans — the association has brought attention to the state of the Casale, an abandoned medieval tower and farmhouse. Aided by partners, including the Regione Lazio — Rome's regional authorities — it has provided lighting, reclaimed the land and, "above all," says Valerio proudly, "connected Colli Aniene and its underground to the neighboring districts by a secure pedestrian path."

"Il Cinema in Piazza," says Valerio, "has become the instrument by which we prompt institutions to attend to common goods." Cinema America is "part of the same process." All their actions aim to "create processes of urban and social regeneration." While they declare themselves firmly anti-fascist, anti-racist and advocates of an inclusive society, they have always tried to be open "to all beliefs, age-groups and social backgrounds." They can project blockbusters and Walt Disney to children at the Cervelletta and, at the same time, invite writers such as Roberto Saviano[4] and directors like Ken Loach.[5] From the start, they "have had a social mission: to reduce social conflicts with culture and cinema, creating opportunities for meeting and discussing [...] to create a real community as opposed to a virtual one."

Still, Valerio and the Foundation have been accused of bowing to the PD, (the center-left Italian political party) a charge they repudiate. As a Foundation, "our aim is to be acknowledged by all institutions, under whatever government," he says.

---

[4] Roberto Saviano is a famous anti-mafia writer.
[5] Ken Loach is a well-known radical British film director.

Disillusioned with Italian politics, his sources of inspiration are elsewhere: the boy-scouts that he joined as a young boy, and his grand-mother, who served on the city counsel for the communist party mayors; Argan, Petroselli and Vetere.[6] When he turned to activism in high-school, she advised him that "the best way of contributing to society was by an effective cultural and community-led intervention." "I am thrilled when I think about Rome today," he says enthusiastically, when he thinks about his "older brother," Pietro Vicari at Quarticciolo Ribelle,[7] whom he met as a schoolchild, and Tommy Salaroli at Scomodo,[8] "who started out at Cinema America." "There is a lot going on in Rome," he says. But he classifies the multitude of Roman grass-root organizations as "heretical experiences" in relation to the Roman and national political panorama.

In 2016, the organization won a public tender to rent Cinema Troisi — another abandoned cinema and architectural monument — designed by the Italian rationalist architect Luigi Moretti in1933. Notwithstanding a myriad of bureaucratic challenges, it was able to raise the necessary funds to refurbish the cinema and reopen it in 2021. One year later, says Valerio, Cinema Troisi was voted the number one Italian single-screen cinema for public attendance, securing an audience of sixty thousand people during the 2021-22

---

[6] Between 1976 and 1979, Giulio Carlo Argan served as the first communist mayor of Rome and was followed by Luigi Petroselli and Ugo Vetere.
[7] Pg: 10
[8] Pg: 18

season, of which sixty per cent were under thirty-five, and of those, seventy per cent were the so-called "streaming generation," the under twenty-sevens. Valerio takes me down to their office to meet Giulia Flor Buraschi, the twenty-five-year-old vice-president of the Foundation,[9] and Federico Croce, the Director General. Valerio is the president. Despite the hierarchical structure, they are adamant that important decisions are made collectively by the assembly, including many of the group's original members, while the every-day running of the organization, including cinema programming, is managed by Valerio, Giulia, Federico and another six members of staff — all under thirty — and all on open ended contracts. A rarity for young people in Italy.

Cinema America's "only flaw was that it was illegal." Cinema Troisi is also a "cinema like any other cinema, but with a space for the community, and a free study-room, open 24/7, three hundred and sixty-five days a year," says Giulia. This elegant black and white, one hundred and fifty square metre open space with a huge terrace, equipped with WIFI, is the only free study-room of its kind in Italy, she tells me. Students from all over Rome now have a home in the historic center. The atrio, dominated by a circular bar, is another popular meeting-place. Cinema Troisi, she continues, "is a source of enormous energy, even on days when we are feeling tired and fed up; to arrive here and find the study-room full, to see all the young people. […] It is a place where everyone feels a sense of belonging." "Compared to politics with a big P, we

---

[9] In 2022, the Associazione Piccolo America became the Fondazione Piccolo America.

are trying to engage in concrete actions on the ground, and for the city," says Federico. "Cinema is a culture service and between free entrance (Il Cinema in Piazza) and subscriptions and discounts (Cinema Troisi), we aim to disseminate culture so that everyone can benefit." The cinema is open all day and evening with a vast programme of mainstream and independent films as well as a series of retrospectives, movies for children on Sunday mornings and horror films and classics late at night.

Recently, Valerio has been able to reduce his 24/7 schedule, escaping to the mountains in August to spend time alone. He seems relieved. "The real victory," he says, "is that I am no longer indispensable, that the experience can survive and surpass its founders." The Foundation's ambition is to open "a wide-spread multi-screen cinema" or "cinema district in Trastevere" by replicating the Troisi model in other cinemas, and "to continue to block property speculation." It is now backed by a group of investors who hope to buy the Cinema America. "It would be their dream to reopen it," he exclaims. Above all, he adds, reappropriating Baden-Powell's[10] motto, his dream is to "try and leave this world a little better than you found it." "That is our mission," he concludes, with a big smile.

---

[10] Robert Baden-Powell was the founder of the Scout movement.

From the left: Tommaso Salaroli (with microphone), Lorenzo Cirino (seated in front), Edoardo Bucci (with glasses - seated left on the sofa), Susanna Rugghia, Francesco Rita, Sara Paolella, Chiara Carbone, Giacomo Fabbri
Photo by Roberta Ungaro, 2023

# Tommy/Scomodo

"Have you seen this? We built this wall ourselves to make a study-room," says Tommaso Salaroli, known as 'Tommy.' A study-room that is packed with students working silently. We are at Scomodo's La Redazione, (editorial offices) "a free space to live in, to build and to protect,"[11] albeit with the cosiness of a friend's home, and a big one: it encompasses two thousand two hundred square meters. At the entrance to the main space, two boys are competing in a ping-pong match. An array of hanging plants trail down from the ceiling, draping over some of the numerous books that line the walls of this huge room. A raised wooden platform stands in the center. In the evenings, it is used for hosting events; this afternoon, it has been adopted by a group of teenagers engrossed in a chess game. Elsewhere, girls and boys are hunched over their computers, perched on chairs around little scarlet red tables, while their companions are reading or chatting quietly, huddled together on a couple of well-worn

---

[11] *Scomodo* No.45

sofas. The soothing sound of a ping-pong ball merges with the music playing at the bar.

I have met Tommy a few times and have yet to see him stand still. "A volcano of energy" is how a colleague described him. He darts gracefully around the rooms, running from one sentence to another. "Look at this, we constructed this as well," he points to a tall bookcase in their offices that reaches up to a mezzanine. We climb up the stairs to find a place to talk. I have not been to La Redazione since it opened over two years ago and during that time — the Covid19 pandemic notwithstanding — the team at Scomodo has transformed its venue beyond recognition. A transformation that is not only physical: they have also rebuilt the organization. "We have grown," says Tommy with a grin. His sharp green eyes twinkle impishly.

In 2016, seventeen-year-old Tommy, together with a school friend, Edo (Edoardo Bucci), founded a printed journal and an organization called Scomodo (Uncomfortable). As the name suggests, the ambition was not to conform to society but to disrupt it by guiding the under 25s away from the web and social media to "slow, independent and critical information." A Generation Z editorial project that defies the internet to offer an alternative model of information was a courageous move and, seven years later, Tommy, Edoardo and their cohorts have not lost their audacity. Two years ago, they had achieved a monthly print run of seven thousand five hundred copies, higher than any other student magazine in Europe; now they are relaunching the journal with a monthly print run of twenty-five thousand copies, "higher than any other student magazine in the world!" exclaims Tommy proudly, "and the journal will be distributed to forty Italian cities!"

Today, a group of sixty young women and men — from a variety of disciplines and social backgrounds — contribute to a periodical produced entirely by the under-30s for the under-30s (and not only). Articles cover a range of issues of particular relevance to Italy's youth: the housing emergency, education, the climate crisis, migration, feminism and the cultural avantgardes, with a section dedicated to emerging artists and prose writers. Texts are long for a peer group accustomed to the distractions of social media, yet the magazine is unequivocally popular; it has a following of nearly one hundred thousand. The website is instrumental in attracting new readers and in supporting the journal; virtual updates to articles are supplied through an infographics system. Enticingly designed, the cover reads €0 in schools and universities, €5 elsewhere.

Tommy's enthusiasm is contagious, but these are bleak times for the young. Some have lost hope. In Rome (and not only) they face unemployment, a cost-of-living crisis and unaffordable rents. Understandably, they feel unrepresented by political leaders. The city lacks public spaces where they can meet and study while bookshops, theaters and cinemas continue to close. Increasingly isolated, many young people only communicate through social media. Not surprisingly, the use of tranquillizers and anti-depressants has skyrocketed. Tommy describes the Scomodo team, all in their twenties, as "nerds, losers, swots and anxious people." We walk down the stairs to meet them. Certainly, they are disarmingly honest about their fragilities: "I never studied anything," says Tommy. "I am shy and don't like public speaking," says the thoughtful Edo. However, "together we can build on these oddities — I think it makes us a little like superheroes," Tommy says jokingly. Acting as "we and not I," they are better able to deal with adversity.

"So, what motivated them to launch the organization?" I ask him. "A real feeling of loneliness," replies Tommy, "and a need to be part of something. A feeling that is shared by others, not only me because we are now a big 'family' of one thousand five hundred, and over ten thousand people collaborate with us." Cinema America[12] was a notable influence. By participating in its events in his early teens, Tommy realized that 'together we could do things seriously' and work collectively on socio-cultural projects. Disenchanted with politics like many of his contemporaries, he took part in student protests. Scomodo was able to turn protest into project: "It is one hundred per cent a community project and a way of practicing cultural politics in the city […] and being together is fun," says Tommy. As in most workplaces, there are tensions but on the whole, the group tells me, divergences are overcome through discussions and collective decisions. Each person has a specific responsibility, and everyone has a voice. They all share a sense of belonging: from Lorenzo, head of finance, and Susanna, editor-in-chief, to Martina, who coordinates the research center, and Agnese, head of human resources and community outreach — and there are many more. "Tommy and Edo may be the strategic directors, but there are no bosses

---

[12] Pg, 14

at Scomodo. It belongs to everyone," says Martina. "And that is why it is not just work for us," she continues, even though they are often in the office from 8:00 am to 8:00 pm as well as on weekends. "We all feel it is a sort of mission," she adds.

Scomodo is a movement that aims to rebuild hope for young people and encourage them to play a more active role in the community. 'There are still pages to be written" reads their new slogan: the new generations can shape society. Scomodo seeks to generate change through two enterprises: the editorial — the journal and the web platform — and the public space: La Redazione, opened in 2020 in the garage basement of Spin Time Labs in the central San Giovanni neighborhood.[13] It is an appropriate location given the collective's concern with the housing emergency. The garage was revamped by young architects (and students) and over a thousand volunteers in a hands-on, participatory planning project. A crowd-funding campaign financed the operation and sponsorship in kind helped furnish the space.

"It is a public space open to everyone," says Tommy, regardless of their political allegiance "as long as they are not

---

[13] Spin Time Labs is a former office building, occupied and self-managed since 2013 by a collective of three hundred and sixty-four residents, composed of twenty-six different nationalities. The collective furnishes accommodation for those in need and hosts twenty-four organizations that provide socio-cultural services for the city. It hit the headlines in 2019, when Cardinal Krajewski broke a police seal to reconnect the electricity. In 2023, Roma Capitale (Rome's Municipal Government) announced that they intended to buy and restructure the building and regularize the occupation, an offer declined by the owner.

fascists. […] There are no structures like this in Rome: a place where young people, from the Pariolino[14] to girls and boys from the city's outskirts, can meet their contemporaries and experiment with ways of sharing a physical space, learning how to exchange ideas and work together as a community." Open from 8:00 am to midnight, hundreds of people pass through every day. It is home to Scomodo's editorial board and fulfils three functions: cultural innovation — hosting talks, concerts, performances and shows by emerging talents —, professional training, and support to Rome's youth, particularly adolescents. The latter was an "unexpected development," says Tommy. Scomodo provides a refuge for teenagers, sometimes acting as an intermediary with psychologists, social workers and even the police when minors go missing. The collective also hosts the Polo Civico (Civic Center) composed of a hundred neighborhood associations and offers an after-school service that assists local schoolchildren with their homework. The team's objective is to open other Redazioni in Italy's major cities, starting with Milan, where it won a public tender to launch a new venue in the San Siro district.

Last year, the collective decided to make the transition from a student venture to an enterprise in "the adult world," as Tommy calls it. An equity crowdfunding campaign financed the launch of Scomodo as a start-up, enabling the team of twenty-seven, plus eight bar staff, to start receiving salaries. The ambition is to remain an independent and self-financing enterprise. To this end, the collective collaborates with

---

[14] The Parioli is a wealthy district in Rome.

seventy-five ethical partners, including Greenpeace and Banca Etica. As CEO and head of strategy execution, one of Tommy's toughest challenges has been to run such a complex enterprise under the constant threat of eviction. There have been times, he says, when he arrives at the traffic lights on his moped and bursts into tears in desperation. However, he adds, he is able to maintain his enthusiasm most days by coming into La Redazione and "seeing people working with optimism to make this a better world — and it's paid work!"

Tommy calls his contemporaries the Peter-Pan generation, but their Neverland is not always an imaginary world. They have witnessed some real-life fairy tales. During the renovation of La Redazione, an unknown guest appeared: a middle-aged woman called Paola who had bought a former metal foundry in the historic center to prevent plans to convert it into a restaurant. She wanted to revitalize the neighborhood by entrusting her space to young people. Impressed by Scomodo's ability to develop critical thinking, she offered to lend the venue to the team, delighted to be able to give them a home where they would not have to worry about being evicted. A home that accommodates Scomodo's research center, where a group of seven independent researchers from a number of disciplines — mainly young women — study the relationship between the new generations and the city of Rome; planning events to disseminate aspects of research that are often inaccessible to their peers while also stimulating debates with older age groups.

In just seven years, Scomodo has taken some big steps, and it has equally ambitious plans for the next six years. Because, when the group reaches thirty, it intends to hand over a "structured and sustainable organization" to the generation below it. "That is our main goal," says Tommy. "It is our responsibility to raise awareness, just by showing the younger generations that it is possible, that there are ways of being and working together and that they can do it too — that they can think and act for themselves […] they can even vote for a right-wing government as long as they are aware, they have read, they are informed." When Tommy launched Scomodo, he spoke about "the dream of creating the city we would like to live in." He rarely uses the word 'dream' anymore, he says, "perhaps because the dream is happening."[15]

---

[15] In 2025, Scomodo will open a huge second space in Milan and is seeking to launch new centers in Empoli (Tuscany) and in Bari (Puglia).

From the left: Laura De Dilectis, Ilaria Saliva, Caterina Fantetti, Bianca Hirata and Beatrice Antonelli (in the front).
Photo by Bianca Hirata, 2023

# Laura/Donnexstrada

Sole, a young student and part-time bar attender at the Cinema Troisi, was the first to tell me about the Punti Viola (Purple Points), 'safe spaces' for women in the city. She was happy that the Cinema Troisi was a Punto Viola. At the time, I was baffled. I had never heard of them, although I had heard about Donnexstrada, the organization that invented them. Curious to learn more, I contacted Laura De Dilectis, the twenty-nine-year-old creator and co-founder of Donnexstrada, who invited me to meet her at the organization's book presentation at Zalib, another Punto Viola in Trastevere and a cultural hub for the young — equipped with a library, a bar and study-spaces.

Laura and I meet at the bar, and she quickly guides me to a table outside in Zalib's luscious garden where we sit down with our drinks. With her angelic face and gentle smile, she looks considerably younger than her age. Still, soon I realize that I am sitting opposite a formidably determined young woman driven by an impressive self-belief. "Everything is possible," she says. "Since I was a child, I have enjoyed resolving problems; if I did not like something, I did not accept it, I changed it." One of the things she does not accept is women's limited freedom in the public space which she considers should be for everyone. "It should be normal for a woman to be able to walk home at three or four am — with a dead phone — without having to worry," she says. I agree it should be taken for granted, of course, but for a woman of my generation it seems like an impossible dream. Yet, Laura is confident that in her lifetime, women will be able to roam freely at night without anxiety. Looking at how much her enterprise has achieved in just two and a half years, I am ready to believe her.

The death of Sarah Everard in London was Laura's alarm bell. In March 2021, thirty-three-year-old Sarah Everard was walking home one evening when she disappeared. She was kidnapped, raped and murdered by a policeman. "It was as if I suddenly grew up," says Laura. She launched a call to action on her private Instagram account. Her idea was simple and effective. "If you are coming back home alone at three am and you don't want to wake up your mother or a friend, you have a hotline to call:" a live video call available on Instagram 24/7. In just three weeks, her followers increased from eight thousand to seventy thousand. In two months, the project went viral. And there were also men among her followers, chiefly from the LGBT community, worried about personal safety at night. Laura was surprised by her own success. It was indicative of how many people feel unsafe on the streets. She teamed up with ten young women: friends and acquaintances from the center of Rome, like herself. "Perhaps we are doing something important," she thought at the time. "We were filling a need." Besides alleviating fear, explains Laura, having an eyewitness testimony also deters potential aggressors. Today, the calls are recorded and, if necessary, the organization's volunteers can contact the police. "It (the service) does not exist in any other country," says Laura proudly. She uses it herself. Never having learnt to drive, Laura relies on public transport. Returning by bus one evening to her home in Monteverde (central Rome), she noticed a group of boys staring at her. They alighted at the same stop. It was a twenty-minute walk home. Laura decided to start her call. "Forget about it," she heard the boys say, "she's on a video call." "Maybe nothing would have happened," says Laura. But at least she could feel secure.

Like many people, Laura was unhappy as an adolescent. She started taking an interest in psychology. "If I had suffered, others are suffering and I want to be there," she says. In 2021, the same year that she registered as a professional psychologist, she set up the non-profit association Donnexstrada with her colleagues, attracted by "the idea of creating a community, of not being alone, of creating something together." The association is run as a collective: its co-founders are its co-directors: Laura, Beatrice Antonelli, Caterina Fantetti, Bianca Hirata and Ilaria Saliva. The role of president is rotated; Laura is currently vice-president. The organization's mission is to promote women's safety on the streets and combat gender-based violence in order to "advance social change and contribute to creating a society free of gender discrimination."¹⁶ "We want to be free, not courageous," is Donnexstrada's slogan.

Meanwhile, the collective has launched a start-up called Viola to manage the video call — Viola Walk Home — and map the Punti Viola. Named after Franca Viola, who, in 1965, became the first Italian women to publicly refuse a reparatory marriage. "Viola is the technological, digital and innovative part of Donnexstrada," says Laura. She acts as the executive director. On standby across Europe, two hundred volunteers, trained by Donnexstrada, operate in eighteen different languages while there is a demand from countries as far away as India and the Yemen. Viola is about to be launched as an app[17]; the idea is that "you can ring from any country in the world. […] it will be wonderful!" exclaims Laura enthusiastically.

Punti Viola are the invention of Greta Martinez, the Spanish co-founder of the collective[18]. Encouraged by the success of the safe places for women near bars and night-clubs in Spain, Donnexstrada expanded on the idea to include a vast network of businesses open to the public: chemists, hairdressers, beauty centers and gyms, as well as bars, restaurants and supermarkets. Women (and not only women) feel protected on a first date in a Viola bar, explains Laura, or

---

[16] donnexstrada.org
[17] The Viola app was launched in December 2023 and is now available across Europe.
[18] Greta Martinez later left the collective.

at a Viola hotel when they visit a new city. Hairdressers and beauticians, she points out, are often the first to hear about incidents of domestic violence; their clients confide in them. Bar attenders and pharmacists are frequently approached by victims of gender-based violence. Nonetheless, in an online survey conducted by Donnexstrada in 2023, ninety-eight per cent of the participants admitted that they would not know how to respond if such a victim asked them for help. Anyone working at a Punto Viola, explains Laura, will know what to do; they have been trained by Donnexstrada. The objective is to raise awareness, to educate people: to "transform a minority into a majority." Then, she believes, our cities will be safer.

As well as making women's lives safer, the collective aspires to promoting woman's well-being. It collaborates with a team of three hundred professionals who train employees at the Punti Viola and also offer psychological support, legal advice, gynecological consultations — pro-abortion doctors only — and guidance from dieticians, at targeted prices. "We are sort of intermediaries," says Laura, between women and victims of violence and domestic abuse and violence refuges. Rome hosts a network of anti-violence centers of which the most famous is Lucha y Siesta (Struggle and Rest). Laura and Ilaria met as interns at the Casa Internazionale delle Donne, (International Women's House) another well-known organization in Rome, founded by a group of feminists in the late 1970s. Decades later, it remains an indispensable center for the promotion of women's rights and culture.

"Unfortunately," says Laura, "it is often the élite that combats gender-based violence." Laura is "against the elite, against those radical environments, often left-wing and bourgeois […] it is too easy to talk about certain things while being completely detached from them," she says. She is more concerned with working on the ground. "We want to activate the ordinary citizen," she says. To that end, Donnexstrada is a business and works in tandem with the private sector. It is financed by donors and those companies that act as Punti Viola, whereas the start-up Viola relies on investors. Certainly, Laura does not suffer from anxiety; she enjoys the speed of start-ups and is stimulated by the world of digital innovation. Social media, she sees as a democratic tool, when handled correctly. She is interested "in taking action, otherwise I would be finishing a PhD," she says laughing. For now, the five co-directors are able to draw salaries but she admits it is a struggle. Laura works ten to twelve hours a day and has no private life. In 2022, she was voted one of Forbes 'Italy Under 30' notable people as well as 'Woman in Business' in the Women of Europe Awards. Her mentors are, perhaps not surprisingly, older women entrepreneurs.

Ilaria and Beatrice arrive, and Laura is whisked away for the book presentation of *Non chiamarmi amore*, a fictional book about three young women, inspired by real-life stories and testimonies, and co-written by the team. The following week, I decide to go to the launch/party of a new Punto Viola at Ostello Bello (Beautiful Hostel) in the leafy and central district of Colle Oppio. On arrival, I succeed in pushing my way through the boisterous throng to locate Bianca, communications and creative director, and Caterina, head of PR and events. We find a quiet spot outside. Seemingly indifferent to their striking good looks, both women speak with revolutionary zeal. We are meeting during a wave of protests following the brutal murder of the twenty-two-year-old Giulia Cecchettin by her ex-boyfriend. Femicides are on the increase.[19] In 2023, eighty-five women per day were registered as crime victims by the Italian police force.[20] In memory of Giulia Cecchettin, five hundred thousand people recently took part in a demonstration in Rome organized by the feminist movement, Non Una di Meno (Not One [Woman] Less). I ask them if they think that there is a growing public awareness about gender-based violence. "Italy is finally waking up," replies Caterina, "that is different [...] but we are getting angrier, we want to change things, everyone needs to be re-educated," she continues. The young men serving at the bar — open 24/7 — are "being re-educated, that will have an impact on the ten thousand people who pass through this hostel every week," she says. Donnexstrada counts on two hundred and forty thousand followers, including a small percentage of young men; a community that is expanding every day. Current programmes include mapping 'safe roads' on the Viola app, sensitizing taxi, bus and tram drivers to recognize gender-based violence, and working with schools to raise awareness among the young.

"There are many different battles," says Caterina. "Putting an end to female rivalry is one of them," says Bianca. The Donnexstrada community is "united, we are sisters in the same struggle and all of us want the same change," agrees Caterina. "Empowering women," is another battle, says Bianca. Not only are they contacted about episodes of

---

[19] Giulia Cecchettin was the 105th victim in 2023.
[20] Report by the Polizia di Stato in 2023. 'Questo non è amore'.

violence or worries about safety, they are also asked for advice on a range of arguments: female sexuality, how to be more assertive at work, panic attacks, etc. "To know that people are aware that an organization exists that they can ring, that they can contact and ask for advice on whatever topic they like, for us this is the biggest victory," she says.

Laura's dream is to "transmit a new business culture" with "Viola mega buildings all over the world: centers for empowerment and women's well-being." Bianca agrees. She is confident that "the community will become bigger and bigger," and hopes "there will be the opportunity for each one of us to bring the community into our lives."

# DREAMS 2

## Culture and Sport

From the left: Matteo Dtecchi, Alessandra Salvatori, Francesca Petrucci, Leonardo Sbardella, Claudia Bernabucci (2024).

# Claudia/Cubo Libro

"Why are you going to Tor Bella Monaca?" asks a friend, "it's not a nice district." My friend's views are probably shared by others of his generation. Constantly denigrated by the media, Tor Bella Monaca — Tower of the Beautiful Nun — has become an emblem of urban decay. But meanwhile, over the last few decades, a counternarrative has begun to emerge.

The neighborhood borders the countryside on the eastern outskirts of Rome, twenty kilometers from the center down the via Casilina. It is characterised by its fifteen-storey, grey cement towers that loom over numerous prefabricated buildings. Conceived in more optimistic times, in the early 1980s, Mayor Luigi Petroselli, saw the creation of one of Italy's largest public housing complexes as a solution to both the capital's accommodation crisis and the rising numbers of illegal settlements in the eastern suburbs. Like other projects at the time, it was planned as an autonomous district, but it was built in haste, basic services were never installed, and its thirty thousand residents continue to live in poorly constructed apartments that are now decaying.

Resilient residents have made headway, however. They have battled to obtain services; they have renovated common areas and advanced a multitude of socio-cultural initiatives to regenerate their neighborhood. Above all, they have worked to destigmatize Tor Bella Monaca's name. Since 2014, the Metro C connects Tor Bella Monaca to the city center in twenty minutes and, in 2023, one hundred and twenty-one million euros of public funds were allocated to regenerating the massive R5 housing complex in the degraded northern zone.

Nevertheless, it remains Rome's poorest district, with some of the highest levels of unemployment and school drop-out rates. Tor Bella Monaca is infiltrated by the local mafia; it is Rome's biggest drug-dealing center.[21] On my first visit, I went to report on the work of LabSU, a multi-disciplinary urban studies laboratory, run by Carlo Cellamare, Professor of Urban Planning at La Sapienza University.[22] I remember feeling intimidated by Tor Bella Monaca's reputation, overwhelmed by the gigantic towers and lost in its desolate open spaces; there is a sense of emptiness in this huge concrete

---

[21] "Criminal economies grow most of all where poverty lies, where they provide a concrete alternative to unemployment, but also offer a way of obtaining social recognition." Carlo Cellamare in Carlo Cellamare and Francesco Montillo, *Periferia: Abitare Tor Bella Monaca*, Donzelli Editore, 2022, pg 14

[22] Carlo Cellamare is an authority on Tor Bella Monaca, with Francesco Montillo. LabSU collaborates with local organizations and institutions to work on urban and social regeneration projects.

neighborhood, particularly in the northern zone.[23] "So, if that's how you felt, how do you think a child feels growing up here?" asks Claudia, co-founder and president of Cubo Libro (Book Cube), whom I meet when I return a year later. This time, I come to the Grotte Celoni Metro station, a short walk away from Cubo Libro in Largo Mengaroni in the livelier southern Tor Bella Monaca.

Largo Mengaroni is the only 'piazza' in the entire neighborhood, or rather, it is a vast space surrounded by trees that flank the huge housing estates. Cubo Libro, a bright blue, reinforced cement cube, dwarfed by a grated metal canopy, is only just visible at the far end. Seeing me look lost, an elderly man advises me to walk there in the shade, by the R8 housing complex, between the trees and the back of the mural-covered El Chentro Sociale TorBellaMonaca.[24] When I arrive, a group of boys are playing basketball, coached by two young men. Claudia is sitting cross-legged inside the tiny- thirty square meter building crammed with books.

Claudia's forceful presence is softened by an arresting smile and dark mischievous eyes that seem to miss nothing. She is someone who weighs her words; words are important to her, she tells me. She is, after all, an educator. I take note. Originally from Pantano, on the eastern periphery of Rome,

---

[23] Francesco Montillo has written about the contrasts between different zones in the neighbourhood in *Un quartiere, almeno due luoghi.* (One neighborhood, at least two locations) op.cit., pg 147.
[24] Founded by residents in the early 1990s, the social center also hosts a bicycle workshop and art and ceramic laboratories.

Claudia came to Tor Bella Monaca to study at the local high school. She takes me round to the back of the building to look at Er Pinto and Yest's[25] red mural painting of a nun: Suor Rita, her high-school religion teacher and a mentor. It is thanks to Suor Rita that she started volunteering with the district's young children, where she met Francesca Petrucci, Cubo Libro's future co-founder. "Had I not volunteered, I would have felt worthless, given what I was experiencing." We walk back inside. "No one is sure what this structure was meant to be," she says. The scheme, financed by EU funds in the 1990s, was never completed; the building was abandoned and eventually taken over by drug-dealers. But then, in 2005, it was occupied by a group of defiant women residents and activists from the El Chentro Sociale — and Tor Bella Monaca's first 'public' library was born. Enzo Fabbro, a local tenant, bequeathed his substantial book collection to the new library and other donations followed. "Soon," says Claudia, "a group of people sharing a love of literature started to gravitate to the building; anyone could come and borrow books."

In 2008, they were joined by Francesca and twenty-one-year-old Claudia who, a year later, founded the cultural association Cubo Libro, as a legal entity. When Claudia started clearing out the building and selecting 'literature of quality', curious four-and five-year-old children came to visit them. "They were Cubo Libro's first beneficiaries," she says, smiling. A games collection was quickly established. Crowdfunding and donations financed Largo Mengaroni's first chairs and tables.

---

[25] Er Pinto is a famous street poet, and Yest is a street artist.

"And what about the drug-dealers?" I ask her, "Weren't they hostile?" "They tested us, they studied us," she replies, "but we are with the neighborhood, it would have been counterproductive for them, and then they understood that we were not interested in them." Although they still operate at night. "Were you never afraid?" I ask, even though it is hard to imagine Claudia frightened of anything. "If you are scared, you don't act, you won't change that situation," she replies briskly. "When I was younger, I would close Cubo Libro at 2:00 am but I was never scared, I always thought that if I screamed, someone would come down. There is a community here."

"Look at how the piazza has filled up!" exclaims Claudia, "A world has opened up outside!" The shrieks of the basketball players are growing louder. Since we have been talking, a crowd has formed in the square; the wooden tables are now all taken. Two elderly women are seated next to a group of children practicing their English in a conversation class. Throughout the afternoon, an endless flow of visitors passes by to see Claudia. Two girls come in to say hello and pick up a box of Mikado from a crate of games. At Cubo Libro, games are shared by everyone, and books can be taken home as long as they are brought back. Next comes H, a young man from Ghana. He comes here "for the books and to be with Claudia." Cubo Libro is a place where he can rest after work, improve his Italian and make friends. "He also volunteers for us," says Claudia. A and P, seven and nine years old respectively, rush in and sit down next to us. Equipped with paper and pencil, they start drawing, pausing occasionally to seek Claudia's advice on their artwork. At Cubo Libro they can "draw, play, dance, eat and have a party," says A. T, a middle-aged resident, joins the party. He hands Claudia the program for the Literature Festival that he is attending on the Palatine. "T is our piazza's grandfather," says Claudia. "Cubo Libro is not only a library," says T, "most of all, it has created a place where children, young people and the elderly can congregate." It builds community. "People who are interested bring other people. […] I have seen children grow up, become parents and bring their own children. No other job repays you like this!" says Claudia. The rewards are enormous, despite the many obstacles and difficulties she has faced along with Francesca.

By coming to Cubo Libro, young people learn how to co-habit the public space. "It is a space that makes space," she continues, "where youngsters have a positive place, where they can congregate and play football instead of taking drugs, where there are adults who they can meet, who are welcoming and can listen to them." 'Libertà di Cultura', 'Libertà di Parola', ('Freedom of Culture,' 'Freedom of Speech) reads the mural by the street artist Aladdin on the front wall. "Books are here; if you want them, you can take them: it is our invitation to culture, we make them seem beautiful and attractive, but you are not forced to pick them up." Cubo Libro offers an alternative, she says, "it allows you to see that there are other possibilities."

Claudia is a volunteer president at Cubo Libro. Along with the other seven all-female partners: Francesca, Lorena, Alessandra, Giada, Carolina, Eva and Noemi, she is assisted by a team of ten professionals and fifteen other volunteers who help run an extensive program of cultural and sport activities, as well as educational laboratories in two local schools. Expenses are covered by public tenders, crowdfunding and donations, and recently, by backing from the Paolo Bulgari Foundation. Funding remains a constant anxiety: "every month we risk bankruptcy," she says.

"For outsiders, I am the one who is doing good things; I am seen as a heroine. But I am not a heroine, if I am here, it's because of a sense of belonging," says Claudia. "Non siamo ne santi ne eroi, la vita ti segna e ti insegna come ha fatto con noi" (We are neither saints nor heroes, life marks you and teaches you as it has done to us), writes Er Pinto. Claudia is visibly irritated by the way Tor Bella Monaca's residents are labelled. "I can give you an infinite list of residents who work to help Tor Bella Monaca. [...] I did not create Cubo Libro, I am just part of the story." A story that is not always heard.

Claudia invites me back the following week, to the street party to celebrate the first stage of Largo Mengaroni's makeover. By the autumn, the entire piazza will be renovated.[26][27] The project is funded by the Fondazione Paolo Bulgari, as part of their educational regeneration programme CRESCO. For now, half of the piazza is paved with a gleaming yellow asphalt; oleanders have been planted, interspersed between

---

[26] The completed piazza was opened in December 2023 and has become a vital public space for the community. There are plans to restore the surrounding pine tree forest.

[27] A participatory planning scheme devised hand in hand with the local community and in collaboration with LabSU. Cubolibro acted as the territorial partner.

freshly laid flowerbeds, and a lighting system has been implemented to increase night-time security. The embryonic form of a skatepark is discernible in the distance. Residents, activists, artists and academics are seated together on rows of orange and red benches that glisten in the afternoon sun; children are cheering on a group of teen-agers jostling on the new multi-coloured basketball court; a crowd has assembled around the children's artworks on display at the El Chentro Sociale. The humming of the cicadas has become deafening; for a moment, I imagine that the sea lies behind the neglected pine tree forest that leads to the R5 building.

"I didn't dream Cubo Libro" reiterates Claudia. "I dreamt how to improve it." Her dream, she says is "to see the piazza full of young people who come here to cultivate their dreams: to become a basket-ball champion or a skater, to write poetry or become an artist, because in this piazza you can see that it can be done. I dream that they can all choose an honest and serene life, and I dream that I no longer see young boys fall into the arms of the mafia or end up in prison, because we have all seen that."

From the left: Sylvia De Fanti, Giorgina Pi.
Photo by Ilaria Magliocchetti Lombi, 2021

# Sylvia/Angelo Mai Altrove

The first feeling you experience at Angelo Mai Altrove (Angelo Mai Elsewhere) is one of being welcomed. Whether by the girl at the gates, the young women at the door checking the Arci[28] passes, the boys serving at the bar, or by other members of the public; anyone who comes to Angelo Mai is made to feel part of a temporary community. Its monthly 'Merende' (tea-parties) invented by the artistic duo Industriale Indipendente,[29] exemplify this spirit. Zoe, my eldest daughter, is a keen participant, and while the public is young and I am probably the oldest person here, at the Merende, (and at Angelo Mai) "no one is left out."[30] Upon entering the building, we are asked to take off our shoes and leave them in a pile by the curtains and entrance to the main room; young men and women rush to deposit coats and

---

[28] An Italian organization for social advancement
[29] Industria Indipendente: Erika Z. Galli and Martina Ruggeri (also known as Bunny Dakota).
[30] Nicola Gerundino, *Industria Indipendente*, op.cit.

bags together with their shoes, confident that no one in this crowd of strangers will steal them. I am reminded of my early childhood in the late1960s, when my mother would drag me along to Love-ins/happenings where people would gather together to dance bare foot, embrace, converse or meditate. This evening, behind the curtains, there is something of that idyllic and playful atmosphere in this alluring room, lined with soft carpets and walls adorned with colorful banners, until I am jolted back to the 2000s when I read the message at the front of a small tent: 'Before Tinder: Before Grindr: There was love at first sight.' A man called Valerio is on stand-by, ready to help anyone interested find their soulmate. And when you are not dancing to the music played by DJ Bunny Dakota, you can be tattooed, have a massage, embellish your hands with henna, or join a long queue for a horoscope reading. Or you can just sit quietly and take everything in, because this is a "a public place where you can take your shoes off, stop, recognize yourself, get confused and start transformations." A space where the "principals of sharing, offering and hospitality shape the artistic practice and the being together." [31]

The following week, on a cold sunny morning, I return to meet Sylvia De Fanti, co-founder of Angelo Mai. It is a scenic thirty-minute walk from the historic center, through the Circo Massimo and past the Terme di Caracalla. When I arrive, Sylvia is standing outside the gates, finishing a phone call with one of her colleagues. With a cascade of auburn hair, a firm gaze and a vigorous handshake, Sylvia receives me

---

[31] Angelomai.org.

warmly, and once inside, we sit down at the bar. She smiles. She has just returned from filming abroad. When she is not busy making a living as a stage and cinema actress, or looking after her family, she co-manages Angelo Mai pro bono, as a second full time job. Sylvia speaks with the clear diction of an actress in a nearly perfect British English, having lived in Hong Kong as a small child. Back at school in Italy, at the age of eleven, she met Giorgina Pilozzi — now known as Giorgina Pi — with whom she became inseparable friends, and eventually, co-founders of Angelo Mai.

That is how it began, she explains, in 2004; the two women were in their late twenties. "Giorgina rang me and said, 'you have to see this place.'" She had joined a group of twenty-five homeless families who had occupied an abandoned boarding school — named after Angelo Mai, a nineteenth-century Jesuit Cardinal — in the Monti neighborhood in central Rome. "It started spontaneously," she says. They were a "band of friends: musicians, actors, directors and artists who saw this incredible space" with a small theater and a stunning deconsecrated church and garden. They started calling other friends; "there is this room, you can rehearse here," she recounts. There was a "big need of free places." Soon classrooms were converted into spaces for rehearsals and workshops where artists could interact and exchange ideas; the theater provided a stage for plays and performances, and concerts and parties would animate the courtyard and garden. The families lived upstairs, some participated; "often we would have dinner together," says Sylvia. As activists, they supported the homeless families and most of all they found a "place for independent culture and the development of creativity" where they could experiment freely and offer public cultural events "accessible to everyone: from intellectual evenings to the World Cup in 2006." Well-known professionals like Vinicio Capossela[32] came and performed for free. A community began to form. But in 2006, they were evicted. "We are the ones who think that it is more ethical to occupy a space than to leave it abandoned," they would later write in their manifesto. Today, the building stands empty and derelict, a festering wound in the center of the city.

For a short period in the early 2000s, the historic center was revitalized not only by Angelo Mai but also by the Rialto Sant'Ambrogio that became another vital center for the production of independent culture. In 2011, when Rome's oldest theater, the eighteenth-century Teatro Valle, was threatened with privatization, it was taken over by hundreds of performing-arts professionals and citizens; Sylvia was one of the squat's co-founders. Its remarkable range of 24/7 culture activities and workshops attracted the attention of the international press, but its biggest achievement was that "we built the foundation of the cultural commons," she says, a third sector, independent of the public and private spheres. Working in tandem with the constitutional lawyer, Stefano Rodotà, Teatro Valle was briefly transformed into the Fondazione Teatro Valle Bene Comune. "Culture is a common good that belongs to everyone," says Sylvia. Teatro Valle was run by ordinary citizens on the principles of "the commons, mutualism and co-working," as well as fair wages

---

[32] Italian musician

for workers and attainable theater prices. Though they were evicted in 2014, "we still did it, we showed that it was possible," she says smiling. Angelo Mai continues to stand by those values; "Keep fighting," remains their motto.

Between 2006 and 2009, when they moved into their new venue, the collective operated as a nomadic enterprise. "We stayed alive by producing two musical albums," says Sylvia, and forming both an orchestra — Orchestra mobile di Canzoni e Musicisti — and a theater company/collective called Bluemotion. The collective, directed by Giorgina, who is also a political playwright and video-maker, combines drama, live music, and visual arts in its productions and presents radical theater at Angelo Mai and elsewhere. It has been responsible for diffusing the work in Italy of both Caryl Churchill, one of Britain's best-known dramatists, and the poet and rapper Kae Tempest, and is the recipient of numerous prizes. In 2016, UBU's prestigious Premio Speciale (UBU prize) was awarded to Angelo Mai.

While the local government had assigned the collective a new location — a former bowling green — the venue had "no real floor, doors, or windows." They inaugurated the space in 2009: "a place to invent the possible." Public funds covered only a part of renovation expenses; "we built the rest through our activities during the following years. [...] It is a homely space," she adds, and home to some of the most innovative independent drama, performance, music and dance events in Italy. From Mariangela Gualtieri, Motus and Balletto Civile to Massive Attack and James Lavelle — just to mention a few — an array of both emerging and established artists has come to perform at Angelo Mai Altrove (Angelo Mai Elsewhere) as it is now called.

"We believe in independent culture, we believe in free culture, we believe in a place accessible to everyone, where with ten euros, you can see a play!" she exclaims. "How do you manage to keep prices so low?" I ask her. "It's a lot of work and it's very tiring," she says, sighing. Notwithstanding twenty years of activity, they have not been able to complete a regularization procedure and so cannot apply either for public tenders or EU funding. They have been faced with eviction twice. Finally, she tells me, last summer (2023), Rome Tribunale (Rome's district court) acknowledged not only the "cultural nature of their work," but also that the "administrative inertia" of the local government had prevented them from achieving legal status. For now, they rely on revenue from the bar and funds from their parties and Merende. "We love our parties," she says, "but we also do them to fund the theater." Today Angelo Mai is a collective of around twenty people with a historic core of friends — family — who grew up together and younger people who joined them later. Regular collaborators form part of the wider collective, says Sylvia. "We all work on the annual programming and each person has a specific role." Officially, Sylvia manages the shifts but today she is also checking the toilets and the garbage; as a result of their uncertain legal status — AMA[33] will not collect garbage. "In a public speech, I said they want us tired," she chuckles. There are times when they are "completely fed up with dealing with all the bullshit." The fight with political institutions she calls "excruciating," and

---

[33] The local government entity responsible for collecting garbage.

has praise only for the previous 5 Star local government. "In twenty years, they were the only ones with whom we were able to establish a dialogue."

"So, what drives you?" I ask her. "We are one of the last strongholds in the city, so I feel I have an ethical obligation to keep all this going," she replies swiftly. "There is an ethical need to raise a future generation." Sylvia is an extrovert and enthusiastic mentor to the young. "Young artists want to grow up here and want to have the tools to do it," she says; she trains the junior staff. Their eagerness also encourages her. "We need to build a sustainable activism," she says. To this end, they strive to arrange assemblies, particularly for Rome's youth. Theater workshops are a regular feature, including a laboratory for actors and directors under thirty-five, as well as one for adolescents, and the elderly are not forgotten: Fotoromanza is a studio run by Giorgina for women over sixty-five. Over the years, they have scheduled summer school drama lessons as well as poetry, photography, dance and performance labs. Sylvia hopes that the "public will become even more mixed and that young people attending the Merende will also attend the plays in greater numbers." And besides the social and peer-group amalgamation, it is also "a place where you can talk with the actors" after the plays, a space where performers and public can meet over a drink. "I have rarely seen such a diverse group of people in one location," I say to her. "Yes," she says, "this place really has that, but I wish it was more; mixing audiences is crucial for a society to live, grow and evolve." Most of all she hopes that Angelo Mai will remain an "artistic, political hub," and that "kids will come in wanting to do something like this elsewhere."

Sylvia looks forward to the day when they will be able to act as a legal entity and so procure more funding, both to increase the number of in-house productions and to provide jobs. Her dream is to establish a "School of Arts for acting and directing, where people will come to teach from all over the world," a community that encompasses the numerous "relationships they have built up over the years. […] I would love that!" she concludes. As her friend Giorgina once said, "What is important is to co-habit, to be many, always. And not to underestimate that strength, something that is different from power."[34]

---

[34] Interview, *Pink Noises*, 2020.

From the left and bottom to top:
Luca Grimaldi, Loredana Calvet, Flavio Orlando, Emanuela Moretti, Alberto Montorfano, Lulù Nuti, Pamela Pintus, Lu.Pa., Jacopo Natoli, Cristiano Carotti, Basak Tuna, Simone Testi, Francesco D'Aliesio, Niccolò Giacomazzi, Gianmaria Marcaccini, Gabriele Silli.
Photo by Federico Pestilli, 2024

# Luca/Post Ex

Luca Grimaldi comes running down the ramp to meet me looking a little disheveled. I am waiting outside the entrance to Post Ex. He is late for our morning appointment and his large brown eyes are apologetic. He had a late night, he admits. We are greeted by the screeching sound of an electric saw that belongs to Sebastian, an Argentinian artist that Post Ex is hosting. Luca guides me around the labyrinthine one-thousand-two-hundred square meter former body shop, now home to twelve artist's studios. Most of his colleagues are away on summer holiday. Papier mâché walls and curtains separating one artist from the other seem to have been assembled ad hoc — to meet the needs of the work rather than to forge boundaries between artists. Sometimes there are no barriers; we walk into one room shared by three painters. Others have carefully constructed more intimate places of refuge — studios within studios and even a studio on wheels. The artists' work could not be more diverse. A decapitated washing machine, an amorphous construction somehow held together by hundreds of solidified teabags, dazzling foam sculptures and ceramics, newspapers dipped in acid, cohabit with paintings of all genres, delicate works on paper and digital photographs. There is an art-school feel to the space, abounding with experimental proposals and audacious schemes. It is a "construction site in continuous evolution," writes Post Ex.[35]

We sit down in two comfy armchairs in Luca's exhilaratingly messy studio. He is working on a series of oil paintings that hang on some makeshift walls. Opposite me is a large painting, ironically called 'Il Trionfo di Salute' (The Triumph of Health). Constructed with bold brushstrokes, giant legs of prosciutto (ham), a chunk of mortadella and rolls of salami encircle a huge glass of red wine. We start to talk in English. Luca's mother is American; he went to art school in Boston and then relocated to Berlin. He was thirty-four when he and his wife decided to move back to Rome. "You become a kind of patriot when you live abroad," he smiles.

Post-Ex is one of many artists' collectives that has been reactivating the Roman art world. Driven out of the city center by high rents, groups of artists in their thirties have moved into empty warehouses and factories in the cheaper city outskirts. "Artists and creatives often transform space into something else," says Luca. Given the quantity of disused buildings in the capital, there are innumerable locations called "ex-something." He continues, "in art,

---

[35] *Post-Turismo,* a Post Ex project, curated by Giuliana Benassi, Forse Edizioni, 2023.

everything is a post-something else,"[36] hence, the name Post Ex. "And what bought you together as a collective?" I ask him. "We have always claimed that we are not a collective," he promptly replies. Post Ex defies categorization. They have called themselves "a co-working," "a production house," "a workshop;" "we are a scene most of all," he says. What unites them is the space and the "influence it has on the work […] and the people who come here; you need a certain mind set to work here."

Pragmatism — a characteristic of their generation — drew them together. A huge site that could be shared by a sizable group of people was more economical than a smaller location for an individual. And they wanted large studios. The pandemic lockdown offered a "window of opportunity" to find empty spaces at lower rents. In 2020, Luca signed a contract with the owner of the garage along with his friends and fellow artists: Lulù Nuti, Eleonora Cerri Pecorella, Gian Maria Marcaccini, Gabriele Silli and Francesco d'Aliesio. They were lucky to find a landlord who was less preoccupied with money and more concerned that his property was occupied; he visits them regularly. The artists set to work revamping "one gigantic room" that had been abandoned for years. Post Ex is hidden at the bottom of a 1980s block of flats in Centocelle (one hundred cells[37]), in east Rome, a gentrifying, residential neighborhood. On one side, it borders the public-housing district, Quarticciolo, while on the other, it sits on

---

[36] Op. cit. Luca Grimaldi, Pg 40
[37] The name is said to refer to an ancient Roman military citadel.

the fringes of the lively Tor Pignattara,[38] home to Rome's Bangladesh community. Centocelle is served by three stops on the Metro C and frequented — increasingly — by the young. As the city's new gastronomy center, it is also a favorite haunt of Rome's foodies, even boasting a review in the New York Times. However, I am visiting Luca in the middle of the summer and today even the lively Via dei Castani has not yet emerged from its Ferragosto[39] slumber. Post Ex is located between the Mirti Metro station and the stunning Centocelle archaeological park.

The artists are motivated by a form of idealism, or rather, a curious combination of pragmatism and idealism. They may dislike being defined as a collective, but they "are tied together by a collectivist idea: we understand the value of sharing ideas," says Luca, as well as providing feedback on each other's work. As a result, their work is evolving fast. Such objectives do not only involve the inhabitants of Post Ex. "In here, it is never just us," says Luca; they encourage other artists to come and go and have constructed a white-cube exhibition space in which they invite artists to show their work. Manifestos are "anachronistic" but there are some rules: Post Ex artists cannot exhibit on site; all decisions — including who is admitted when someone vacates his/her studio — are taken in a collective vote during weekly meetings. "We choose the artists who come here well," says Luca, to encourage a diversity of research that helps stimulate dialogue. "Post Ex is also like a 'family,'" he continues, with all the tensions and conflicts that exist in every family. "It is a joy

---

[38] Pg 72.
[39] August 15th, Feast of the Assumption and an Italian national holiday.

to come here every day!" he exclaims. Luca certainly seems like someone who thrives on being with others, although "there is no privacy," he adds. Whenever he is in need of that, he works at night.

There is nothing new either about artists' collectives or artists relocating to poorer districts. What is new is the large number of these collectives in Rome. Luca's generation, he tells me, grew up with a "broken promise of individualism;" the concept of the artist as a solitary genius who would make vast amounts of money. His generation is under no such illusion. Without public support, it is up to them "to help make the Roman art scene grow" — the more dynamic the scene, the more people will benefit. He may be "naïve," he says, but he believes that where there are limited opportunities for everyone, there is a stronger sense of solidarity; artists are united in a common goal. "Rome is a city where contemporary art is not considered," he says; public authorities on both sides of the political spectrum "tend to focus on enhancing cultural heritage." He grew up with "the leitmotiv, you can't do anything here because it's Rome. […] As soon as someone has a bit of optimism, it's contagious," he says. Countries with strong institutions suffered during the pandemic, whereas in cities where "stuff already wasn't working, there were possibilities." "Here, the art scene exploded," he says. In 2020, during a draconian pandemic lockdown, eight artist-run spaces opened in Rome. "Romans," says Luca, "are used to *arrangiarsi da soli*" (getting by on their own). Artist cooperatives have suggested a new way forward. Organizing their own exhibitions and producing publications, they have lured museum curators, critics and dealers to areas of

Rome where they had never ventured previously. [40] "Most of the artists at Post Ex," says Luca, "are now represented by galleries, some of whom are international."

"East Rome is the center for anyone with a VAT number," he says, including a multitude of artists, actors, and musicians. "What is the center? It's a question that as Romans we have to ask ourselves," he continues. When Luca and his wife searched for a flat to rent during lockdown, they discovered that on Airbnb in Rome's historic center, thirty thousand apartments stood empty, without the tourists to whom they were normally rented. A neighborhood, inhabited by only thirty per cent of the local population, was deserted. "An enormous museum with gift shops, English signs, refreshment corners, and information points that had suddenly become useless,"[41] wrote Luca. Many people lost their jobs. "Are we the waiters of Northern Europe? […] Are hospitality and gastronomy all we do?" asks Luca earnestly. Post Ex decided to act, teaming up with the art critic Giuliana Benassi. Between December 2021 and February 2022, twenty — mainly Rome-based artists — converted three empty Airbnb apartments into temporary homes for contemporary art. Romans reappropriated the historic center. Not surprisingly, Post Ex called the project *Post Turismo* (Post Tourism). Expenses were covered by sponsorship from the Regione Lazio.

---

[40] *Vera, Roma, 8 spazi, 54 studi*, conceived by Damiana Leoni and published by Quodlibet in 2021, maps eight artist-run spaces across the capital: a total of fifty-four studios. In 2021, Rome's Galleria d'Arte Moderna celebrated their work in a group exhibition.
[41] *Post Turismo,* op.cit. pg 40.

"While the cooperative may be shaping an artistic community, what about their relationship with the local community?" I ask him. "We are not a social center," he clarifies, much as he admires Forte Prenestino, Centocelle's famous social center that he frequented for decades. Their ambition, he says, is to expand Rome's art scene by raising awareness and by giving younger people opportunities that were not available when they were growing up. To this end, Post Ex collaborates frequently with local schools; many of the artists are teachers. "If the one fifteen-year-old freak in his class comes to a place like this, maybe he will be emboldened to continue as an artist," he says.

I return a few weeks later. Music is blaring; the artists are back at work, and I am welcomed by Lulù Nuti, a young woman with the aura of an actress. Co-founder of Post Ex, Lulù is a well-known sculptor. We sit down with Luca to continue the discussion in her studio. "We are not political in the old-fashioned way — we have not written a manifesto — but we are very political in what we do: there is no boss here, we all represent Post Ex," she says. It is an "attitude, a way of being with others […] we always send someone different to present Post-Ex," she continues. It was Luca's turn when I visited. "Having an idea and sharing it with others, that is political." The first action taken by new artists when they arrive at Post Ex is to add their contacts to the database so that they can be shared, she says. And they are not alone. Lulù tells me about collectives of artists and curators even younger than them. Today, she says, there is an underground artistic and musical scene that is as vibrant as it once was in the 1970s. But it has yet to gain recognition abroad. Luca agrees and dreams that this new 'Rome scene' will become international as it used to be, "when artists and creative people came from all over the world to boost the creative energy of this place." Most of all, Post Ex's goal is "to make Rome fashionable for what it is today and not for what it was in the past."

In the centre: Massimo and the girls and boys at Calciosociale.
Photo by Giovanni Canitano and Roberto Nistri, 2020

# Massimo/Calciosociale

I am standing in a big circle, with some fifty boys — and a handful of girls — together with their fathers, mothers and coaches, in the middle of a football pitch at Corviale, on the south-west outskirts of Rome. A group of teenage boys in uniforms have arrived from the Istituto De Merode in central Rome — a school for the wealthy. They are welcomed by the local kids amid curiosity as to why they are "dressed like Harry Potter." Natalia, Head of Projects, at the organization Calciosociale, announces 'Conflict' as the theme that these aspiring footballers will be studying this year. "That's a difficult word!" exclaims a nine-year-old boy standing next to me. "Don't you sometimes argue with your friends?" asks Natalia, "that is conflict." She proceeds to recite the names of the football teams: words that describe "ways of defeating conflict." "Perseverance," she says. "What is that?" asks a young child. "We train every day, we persevere in our training," explains a coach. "Listening," continues Natalia. "Listening, Dad, do you understand?" jokes an adolescent boy with his father. Children and parents then assemble in mixed teams and this unusual football game begins. An indoor workshop is taking place simultaneously; young children divided into two teams — assisted by an educator and a psychologist — are assiduously writing down their own interpretations of the themes. Outside the entrance, I meet a mother, Sonia di Traglia, chatting with Massimo Vallati, the founder and head of the enterprise, who has just arrived. Massimo is warm and welcoming but sitting down he seems restless. With his lean, agile physique, and his seemingly inexhaustible energy, I imagine him more at home on the soccer field.

One evening in 2005, twenty-eight-year-old Massimo, together with his friend Antonio, rewrote the rules of Italy's most popular sport over a plate of pasta al pesto. They called the new game Calciosociale. Massimo, a television photography director during the day, devoted his spare time to his work as a catechist in a parish in Monteverde in central Rome. Competitive and aggressive football tournaments were "were not compatible with the ideals of justice" they were promoting in the parish, he told me. He promptly proposed his new rules to the local priest. The rules include: anyone can participate between the ages of ten and ninety-nine — girls and boys of all races and religions, including the disabled; all teams have the same number of "technical coefficients," there is no stronger team; there are two educators in every team; there is no referee, every player must learn to be responsible (disputes are resolved through collective decisions); no one can score more than three goals in one match but must help their team score; penalty kicks are taken by the least strong player; matches are not only played on the football pitch, teams must also score points in community activities. The aim of this inclusive game was "to change the rules of football to change the rules of the world."

The game proved successful. Various tournaments were played. Massimo set up an association and started to look for "a home where their project could grow." Rather than teach only well-to-do children, Massimo longed to help poorer families who could not afford to pay for their children's sports activities. When he learnt about an abandoned sports center in Corviale, belonging to ATER, he seized the opportunity to move the game there, even though his colleagues and friends strived hard to discourage him, concerned by Corviale's reputation as a tough neighborhood. Massimo was undeterred.

Corviale is arguably one of Italy's most controversial post-war public housing schemes. Revered by a large number of architects, it is abhorred by an equally large number of residents. *Il Serpentone* (the Big Snake), as it is called, stretches nearly one kilometer in a straight line; a colossal, brutalist building looming over the countryside. But there is nothing sinuous about a construction made up of seven hundred and fifty-thousand cubic meters of reinforced concrete condensed into sixty hectares. This monolithic horizontal skyscraper is formed by a twin structure — thirty meters high — connected through labyrinths of elongated passageways, external corridors and inner courtyards. It can house up to six thousand people, although, over time, its population has diminished considerably.

Inspired by modernist dreams of utopian architecture, the architect Mario Fiorentino designed Corviale in the early

1970s, as a city within a building where collective interests would triumph; an autonomous structure in which the fourth floor would act as a communal high street, furnishing services and commercial facilities for the whole collective. Unfortunately, when residents moved in, ten years later, the building had not been completed; it lacked basic services, communal spaces, and adequate public transport. In a very different political climate, public authorities abandoned Corviale and residents were left to fend for themselves. The empty fourth floor was soon occupied by homeless families. The infrastructure began to deteriorate and Corviale became a symbol of urban decay.

There has been progress, Sonia tells me: tenacious residents have managed to secure numerous services and amenities, and the last fifteen years has seen a proliferation of citizen-led, socio-cultural associations. Today, Corviale is an agreeable — if long — ride on the 98 bus from central Rome. T-Studio architects has designed the scheme to requalify the fourth floor to provide legal accommodation, while fourth-floor residents (and not only) are supported by a unique research laboratory — Laboratorio Città Corviale — run by Roma Tre University; Laura Peretti Architects will be restructuring the ground floor (work has yet to begin), and, in 2023, sixty million euros of public funds (Italy's PNRR/ EU Next Generation funds) were allocated to help regenerate Corviale.

Still, for now, living conditions are harsh, and structural defects in the building are commonplace. "Apartments are falling apart," says Sonia. Sonia was fifteen when she moved to Corviale; she was one of its first tenants. Her parent's generation, who moved there in the early 1980s, are now in their eighties, confined to their flats when lifts break down (frequently) and preoccupied by safety issues at night. Unemployment rates are higher than the city's average and teenagers continue to drop out of school.

"Look at this," Massimo points at the building. To live in Corviale is "to live in a prison." And yet, not only did he bring Calciosociale to Corviale, he moved there with his wife and children. It all began with his passion for soccer, he tells me, "football was my family." But already as a child, he was aware of the "dual experience of the game." While his football club in Portuense, his home neighborhood in west Rome, offered a nurturing environment, he was troubled by the violence and racist attacks he witnessed in the stadium. Massimo was a Lazio-ultras. He abandoned the game at sixteen and later enrolled in the police force, where, by a twist of fate, he found himself on duty in the stadiums, having to control the supporters with whom he had grown up. Disillusioned, he left the police and eventually went into television. Massimo has been an activist since he was fifteen. Activism has enabled him to "channel tensions, anger, indignation and suffering; you can transform it into poison, something that hurts you, or you can transform it into love and positive energy that can be good for you and can also be good for others. [...] You should never trust anyone who tells you they just want to help others, those people are dangerous," his eyes twinkle. For someone who has weathered so many storms, Massimo has retained a mischievous sense of humor.

He continues his story. In 2009, he arrived at Corviale on a contract with the Regione Lazio and two thousand five hundred euros in the association's bank account; they needed five million euros to renovate Fiorentino's derelict sports complex opposite the main building. Massimo and his cohorts quickly moved in to act as custodians of the abandoned building which had been adopted by drug-dealers. Residents, perhaps understandably, were suspicious of these unknown newcomers. Nobody believed that they would be able to revolutionize the site in just a few years. Through crowdfunding, in-kind sponsorship, donations, and some big sponsors, the association raised enough funds to start construction in 2012. "When you come here, there are two things I don't want you to see: grey and cement," says Massimo. And so, in 2014, they opened the new sports complex: a wooden structure with a bright red interior, a geothermal-powered seven-hundred-and-fifty square meter gym and Calciosociale's offices. Two new soccer fields: the Campo dei Miracoli (Miracle Soccer fields) were inaugurated with a symbolic match during FIFA's world cup trophy tour. "The Campo dei Miracoli could only be born here," says Massimo. "It made more sense."

But a year later, Massimo was woken up abruptly in the middle of the night by a "strange red flickering light;" when he ran to the window to open the blinds, he saw that the wooden hut[42] next to their building was in flames. Massimo, his wife and young children were living above the Calciosociale offices. It

---

[42] A hut called the Casetta della Spiritualità open to all religions (the House of Spirituality).

was an arson attempt, and they could all have lost their lives. "The event simply strengthened my resolve," says Massimo, with a smile. A night-time radio, from midnight to 7:00 am — *Radio Impegno* (Committed Radio) "the radio that never sleeps" — was set up to protect the Campo dei Miracoli; citizens across Rome came to Calciosociale to express solidarity and participate in its live transmissions. Massimo coined Calciosociale's slogan: "Vince chi custodisce" (The one who wins is the one who protects).

Today, Massimo heads a team of twelve, assisted by a group of energetic mothers. Over two hundred young people regularly take part in Calciosociale's activities, as do their parents. Seventy percent are residents at Corviale and fifty percent do not pay subscriptions, says Massimo. Nominal fees are calculated on income. Traditional football is also taught — Miracoli FC is a registered football club — and "you can see the difference Calciosociale has made," says Angelo, one of the coaches. "The players treat each other with more respect." It teaches the young to become "active citizens, both on and off the pitch," says Massimo. "I play football, and I learn about the constitution; I play football, and I develop a civic conscience […] it is about raising awareness. […] Look at this," he points to the parking lot, "it was a rubbish dump — the boys and girls cleaned it up during community activities." The association aims to help keep Corvale's youth in school; after school laboratories provide children with assistance with homework; psychologists offer support. "It has been a lifeline for Corviale," says Sonia. "It's our Neverland; a place where young people feel safe." And she can see the change. Her twelve-year-old son Giordano is more confident. "Boys and girls who would hang their heads and were timid and insecure last year, seem much more self-assured this year; they hold their heads high, they learn how to confront problems and how to share things with each other," she says. Francesco, a young boy I meet with her, loves the *divano sociale* (the social sofa): once a week, children and their parents unite for a meal cooked by William, a young local chef. "You can make friends at Calciosociale," says Francesco. "It is a community," says Sonia, and a way of meeting people from other districts.

Massimo explains that he has two objectives: the first is to help the neighborhood: children and their families. The second is "to transform ten thousand Italian football schools into schools of life; football could be the biggest civic education classroom in the country," he says. "At Corviale you can plant a seed, but I am aware of the limits." For a moment, Massimo seems weary. He complains about the lack of public support. So much depends on him. "My dream," he says, "is to construct something that does not rely entirely on me; something that is scalable and replicable, something that you can develop everywhere, all over the world." Meanwhile, his methodology is spreading across Italy and Northern Europe. In 2014, the Italian Government acknowledged Calciosociale as the "best practice" in sport and in the promotion of social inclusion. Calciosociale is "a place that expresses hope, trust and real social growth,"[43] said Sergio Mattarella,

---

[43] President Sergio Mattarella's speech, 22/02/2022

the Italian president, when he came to Corviale to open Calciosociale's third football field.[44]

---

[44] In 2025, Calciosociale built a supporters' stand as part of an extension to the stadium. The idea is to introduce a 'new culture of shared emotions' among supporters of opposing teams who will all sit together. Meanwhile, Massimo has been placed under police escort following threats from organized crime organizations operating in Corviale.

# DREAMS 3

## Urban Landscapes

From the left: Maaty, Francesco and Hamasa (in front with this dog).
Photo by Francesca Castaldo, 2023

# Francesco/Termini tv and Mama Termini

Francesco Conte has given me an appointment at the Obelisco di Dogali, a monument to the five hundred Italian soldiers killed in the Battle of Dogali in 1887, when Italy attempted to establish a colonial Empire in Eritrea. Across the road, the Termini train station soars above the Piazza dei Cinquecento (Square of the Five Hundred). Nowadays, this vast piazza is one of the main arrival-points in Rome for Italy's immigrants. Francesco appears and greets me hurriedly; he is more concerned with taking photos of the barriers around the Obelisk which has been cordoned off during renovation work on the piazza.[45] Francesco is tall and athletic and has a long stride; I struggle to keep up with him. Eventually, we sit down in a café where we are joined by Alice, his colleague and partner.

---

[45] The Roman architecture practice IT's designed the scheme to renovate Piazza del Cinquecento. its.vision/works/piazza-dei-cinquecento/

Every day, around half a million people transit through Termini, Italy's biggest train station. Its distinctive atrium framed by a sloping roof — an extension to the building designed by Eugenio Montuori and Leo Calini and inaugurated in 1950 — is affectionately called the 'dinosaur' by the local population. The ancient Roman Terme di Diocleziano (Baths of Diocletian) stand opposite the station, although the view of this grand monument is partly obscured by the bus and metro transport hub in the center of the square. For many Romans, Termini is a place that you pass through quickly and preferably without stopping; a place that is not considered safe. The "group mentality of Romans is tied to a neighborhood," says Francesco, "usually the one where they grew up. While there are no official residents, Termini is the 'neighborhood' for whoever is not from Rome, and for whoever does not have money to go to the bar." It is his neighborhood and that of numerous immigrants and foreigners.

Francesco arrived from Ancona ten years ago, with his one-year-old son. He was a thirty-year-old unemployed video-maker and knew only two people in the entire city. "I did not know where to go at night," he says, so he would spend time at Termini, near his home; "the only place where I did not feel alone […] a piazza where I could meet people," he says. Meetings were facilitated by his gregarious personality, and in only a short time he was introduced to Angela Cocozza who ran Termini Underground, a dance school for young immigrants, located beneath a train platform in a former after-work space for railway men. Francesco was intrigued. In 2014, he started filming the young dancers and assembled a team of eight "fellow unemployed videomakers, photographers and journalists." There was only one Roman in the original gang. "We were a group of people who did not have a group," he says. Francesco and his cohorts soon realized that there were many stories to be told at Termini, not only about the dancers. "Termini tv (an online TV channel, also on Facebook and Instagram) was born to film the stories of others," he says. And they also hoped that Termini tv would help them find paid work. Eventually it did.

When the mainstream media prefers to report on "degradation and crime" at Termini, Francesco is inspired by Speakers' Corner in Hyde Park in London, where citizens, from all walks of life congregate every Sunday. Anybody can take the podium and talk about whatever comes to mind. In some ways, Termini tv is a virtual Speakers' Corner. The videos give a voice to individuals across the social spectrum: young immigrants, middle-aged Italians, Roma women, musicians, the homeless, commuters, prostitutes, tourists. "Termini is the only authentic place in Rome," comments a busker in one of the videos. It is a microcosm of contemporary society.

In nearly ten years, over one thousand five hundred videos have been produced, of which four hundred are online. Notwithstanding the changes: in 2016, following the terrorist attack the previous year at the Bataclan theater in Paris, barriers were erected to control access to train platforms, explains Francesco. Then local shops started closing down, and the big brands moved in; Termini became a shopping-mall. More barriers were erected to prevent the homeless sleeping outside the entrance. It became more difficult to film. Francesco initiated a program of artistic interventions to appropriate the public space and encourage interaction: poetry recitals, performances by artists and musicians, even horoscope readings. A group of regular participants began to form.

The aim of Termini tv is to teach people to "look at Termini with new eyes, and not just see it as a 'non-place' to pass through," he says. We take a tour. Builders are laying cobblestones as work advances on the refurbishment of the piazza. "More feet and less wheels," is Francesco's summary of the architects' project. He hopes that the new green, pedestrian square will encourage conviviality. "Termini is the only place in Rome where the rich and poor share the same pavement," he laughs. Bodyguards stand waiting for their client outside an armored car; a meter away, two Nigerian men watch them, perched on their makeshift cardboard beds. Francesco greets them. He is 'at home'. He waves at an aged Italian man sitting in front of the entrance. "He has been here for fifty years," he says. "The piazza is divided up by nationality," explains Francesco, "and each national group resents the other as one does in a family," he smiles. On Thursdays and Sundays, carers' and domestic helpers' days off, Peruvians gather on the left side of the piazza. Romanians are on the right. We walk past a group of young Egyptian boys. "The young seldom stay long," he says, "they usually go North, hoping to find work." Nigerians congregate on Via Giolitti on the right side of the building. In the station upstairs, we shake hands with S, a gentle former welder who has fallen on hard times. "He is one of numerous separated men who find themselves living on the streets," says Alice. Termini houses a big community, explains Francesco. Here, people "do not feel judged," and not only Italy's immigrant population. Lonely elderly men, from Rome's outskirts, meet up at Termini. They are unable to live on their dwindling pensions, he informs me. Others are without a pension at all, having had to work off the books all their lives. Then there are "non- violent thieves," as he calls them, male and transexual prostitutes, drug dealers who target tourists and foreign students, and "crazy people."

With imposition of stringent pandemic lockdown restrictions in 2020, the number of volunteers assisting the destitute and homeless declined rapidly. Undeterred by the constraints, Francesco joined forces with the Egyptian journalist Maaty Elsandoubi to launch Mama Termini, an organization to help the vulnerable. They have kept going. Every Sunday at 7.30 pm, Mama Termini and Termini tv host a dinner/party that is open to everyone. Volunteers bring home-cooked food and pizza, Maaty prepares kilos of Egyptian rice, and a couple of Tunisian and Syrian restaurants send supplies of spicy pasta. "Mama Termini has become the container for Termini tv," says Francesco. In the warmer months, he continues to invite musicians and artists to perform. At present, around one hundred and forty people attend Mamma Termini. "It is also a community for us," says Alice. We decide to meet there the following Sunday.

On the coldest Sunday of the year, I reach Termini to see a crowd assembling around the team of thirty volunteers who are setting up the tables on which food will be served.

A commuter passing by to catch a train, could mistake some of the hundred or so men — and the handful of women — gathered here, for fellow travelers. Instead, they clutch heavy bags and suitcases that contain every single item they possess. Maaty and Francesco arrive, loaded with heavy containers of pasta, water, plastic plates and forks. The dinner begins. For a few hours Termini's community comes together to participate in one of the oldest human rituals: the sharing of food. I take in the babel of languages: Italian, Arabic, Somali, Romanian. P, a middle-aged Sicilian man greets me. I am a new face. "He knows everything there is to know about Termini," says Michele, an enthusiastic volunteer who is distributing the pizza. Soon, I meet the jovial A from Romania, T who fled from Bosnia during the war, Sega from Mali, one of the first volunteers, and X, an Italian retired schoolteacher who comes to have a meal and pass out sweets to the volunteers. Silvia, a young helper, introduces me to Shevan, an elegantly dressed Kurdish journalist: having found work, he has crossed to the other side of the table to join the helpers. The large square is temporarily reanimated; the mood is festive. Jokes are exchanged but occasional outbursts of anger can cast a fleeting cloud. There is not always enough food for everyone. Still, "when someone's temper flares, a conational will always come and calm him down," says Francesco.

"The fact that Maaty is Egyptian," says Francesco, "has helped Mama Termini gain the trust of Arab and African immigrants. In three and a half years," he says, "he has only missed three Sundays." Maaty is the Buddha of Termini. His composed, charismatic presence is reassuring; his voice is at times so soft that it is barely audible. He welcomes each person with the warmth of an old friend; he shares the melancholia and adversities of enforced exile. Maaty was introduced to Francesco by a mutual journalist friend he had met in Tahir Square, during the Egyptian Revolution in 2011. He had been eager to take part in the revolution, returning to Egypt from Italy where he had lived and worked for many years. However, when Abdel Fattah Al-Sisi took power in 2014, he was compelled to flee back to Italy. Piazza dei Cinquecento, says Maaty, is like another Piazza Tahir; here too, he combats social injustice.

"We are the only secular organization on the ground here," says Francesco. "What distinguishes Mama Termini from the other organizations that operate at Termini, is its aim not only to "help people but to construct relationships.'" Maaty agrees: "It's not about Italians helping immigrants," he says, "the association is multi-ethnic […] we are not donors, we are friends and family, it's a gathering. (…) Anyone from any country can meet, talk, and also argue," he says, smiling. Maaty has coined the term 'senzatutto'[46] (without everything) for the immigrants at Termini. "They have nothing," he says. Deprived of a roof over their heads, they have "no friends, no family, no-job, no money and no language." They are disregarded and disdained by society. But at Mama Termini, "we eat as we eat at home, you can feel human again […] there is not only a need for food, but also to be together." Maaty's eyes glisten. Here, they realize that "there is still hope, there is someone who understands and someone who will give you

---

[46] A play on the word 'senzatetti' which means 'without a roof', or homeless, in Italian.

a smile." T, an elderly Moroccan lady "was angry and hostile at first, but all she wanted was company, someone to listen to her, and a number to ring," says Alice. "Not everyone is homeless," adds Francesco. There are those who come to ask advice on how to make a life for themselves: how to file for residency permits, how to learn Italian, how to find work. "At Mama Termini, we guarantee safety with kindness," he says.

Francesco has a dream that he admits is utopian: to construct "a hostel in the piazza for artists, mad people, the homeless, and travelers." Only then can you "really help people," he says. But T has "a more feasible dream […] a social and free campsite where anyone can set up a tent."

From the left: Gigliola Cultrera, Lavinia Palma (2024)

# Gigliola/Libera Repubblica di San Lorenzo

"You must meet Gigliola Cultrera," urges Alessandro, an activist at the squat Communia, in the neighborhood of San Lorenzo. "She is a pillar of the community," he told me.[47] Some months later, Gigliola and I arrange to meet at Giufà, a bookshop and café, off the Piazza dell'Immacolata. Our telephone conversations had been formal. I knew that Gigliola was a former Italian and history teacher, now retired; I had watched her eloquent interviews on YouTube. So I was expecting someone a little severe, possibly intimidating, and am surprised (relieved) to see this seemingly gentle middle-aged lady approach me with her eyes scrunched up in a friendly smile. We are welcomed by her friend, Francesco Mecozzi, the co-founder of the bookshop. Giufà encourages browsing, books are displayed at varying heights and angles so that anyone at any age can find something to read. Gigliola directs me to

---

[47] I met Alessandro with Emilia Giorgi, another prolific activist, who introduced me to number of San Lorenzo's collectives.

the bar where we sit down to talk, quietly. At the next table, students are studying.

San Lorenzo is a neighborhood I visited frequently when I arrived in Rome as a student in the early 1980s. Forty years later, it is almost unrecognizable. Built in the late nineteenth century to accommodate a working-class population of artisans and rail- and factory workers, there is a gritty feel to the district, defined by the monuments of its industrial past and buildings that still bear the scars of Allied bombing during WWII. This small territory is wedged between Termini, the main train station, Verano, the monumental cemetery, and the Città Universitaria La Sapienza (La Sapienza University). In the 1960s and 1970s, San Lorenzo was home to radical left-wing and student groups. Artists and writers began to move in. Soon, bars and restaurants opened to attract the young. AirBnbs and tourists followed; property prices and rents escalated, and artisans and many local residents were forced to move out. It is a common story. Today, San Lorenzo is a center of Rome's nightlife. Meanwhile, developers have bought up land. Many have constructed expensive apartment and office blocks, while others wait and allow empty buildings to decay.

Property speculators are interested in San Lorenzo, explains Gigliola, "both because of its central location between Rome's two principal railway stations: Termini and Tiburtina, and because it still has stretches of unused land with abandoned warehouses and workshops. […] It is an area where you can build in abundance," she says. "It is always presented as 'requalification' but, in reality, it is speculation." "Still," she continues, "two visions of the city" co-exist here. Over the last few decades, a multitude of self-financed citizens' cooperatives has emerged to build what they call a "a possible (building) site," based on a system of mutual aid. In opposition to speculation and privatization, they have reappropriated and renovated disused buildings, restoring them to the community to promote independent culture and offering services that include an adolescent psychology support center called Il Grande Cocomero. (The Big Watermelon.)

Gigliola took up residence in San Lorenzo in the late eighties. She was happy to move to a more central neighborhood near the University Psychology Faculty with whom she collaborated. In the early 2000s, a project by La Sapienza University to redevelop the Vetrerie Sciarra (Sciarra Glassworks) next door to her home prompted her interest in activism. When Gigliola and her neighbors discovered planning errors in the scheme, they created a group to oppose the project and mediate with the local municipality. For the first time, she says, she "experimented with community solidarity, a force that could exert pressure on institutions." They were able to modify the scheme but not prevent it. Some years later, residents near the Ex Fonderie Bastianelli (Bastianelli Foundry) "asked for local solidarity" to protest against a private developer's demolition of a listed building. While the community lost the battle, a grassroots association of residents and activists was formed; it called itself the 'Libera Repubblica di San Lorenzo' (Free Republic of San Lorenzo). Gigliola was one of the founding members. Determined to compensate for the "incapacity of the local government"[48] and to battle for public spaces and services, the "Libera Repubblica coordinates the vast network of collectives and individuals. Its strength," she says, "is the range of different ages, personal histories and cultures."

She takes me to see what has become of the foundry. Ten years later, the project to build a luxury apartment block remains uncompleted; apartments are still vacant. "Construction in Rome is dominated by private sector interests [...] the interests of the few who make profits prevail at the cost of increasing inequality (...) It is hard to litigate against developers," she explains, "because of the constant name changes of the owner, one company disappears and another appears," and often, she goes on, "things move so fast that by the time one is able to appeal, it is too late." A case in point is another building site we walk past, where a tall construction has been erected in the middle of a courtyard, blocking the view of adjacent low-rise apartments. Gigliola describes the new ten-story building — Soho House: an exclusive club for 'international creatives,' — as emblematic of these urban transformations. "Developers and entrepreneurs," she explains, "like to exploit San Lorenzo's reputation as an authentic and creative district; it is sold as a brand."

Gigliola methodically recounts a series of failed attempts to block developers. She speaks softly and seems unperturbed. "What drives you to continue?" I ask her. She smiles. "At a time when politicians struggle to establish a presence on the ground, these entities (grassroots associations) are the

---

[48] Manifesto della Libera Repubblica di San Lorenzo.

only ones making an impact. It is rewarding to be to be an active part of a collective vision committed to a different idea of the city." We stroll to the walled-up Nuovo Cinema Palazzo (New Cinema Palazzo) in Piazza dei Sanniti, which has remained a symbol of the 'site of the possible', even though its occupants were evicted in 2020. In 2011, a group of residents, activists, and performing artists took over the former cinema to prevent a private developer converting it into a casino. For the next decade, volunteers and professionals provided not just San Lorenzo but the entire city with a rare experimental music and theater hub, hosting readings and debates as well as after-school laboratories for children and adolescents, and events for the elderly. Initiatives, she tells me, that would transform the building and the piazza "into a public space for the neighborhood, a place of real socialization." Years later, the building stands empty.[49]

Cinema Palazzo was also the headquarters of the Libera Repubblica. It now meets less regularly at Esc. "Esc is active at so many levels," says Gigliola, enthusiastically. Founded over twenty years ago by a group of students from La Sapienza, it holds cultural events and assemblies and is equipped with a bevy of self-managed information desks run by volunteering professionals. Support is available to immigrants and women victims of discrimination and violence, and a labor union offers free legal assistance. Aided by a crowdfunding

---

[49] The 5Star local government tried unsuccessfully to buy the building. In January 2024, the owners announced that the building will be rented to a group of young businessmen.

campaign, Esc has been able, for now, to avoid eviction by the local administration.

It is not possible to visit all the different grassroots associations that operate in San Lorenzo in one long morning; there are simply too many. Gigliola takes me to see the grounds of the Atletico San Lorenzo. The Cavalieri Di Colombo (The Knights of Columbus), an American Catholic organization, granted the Atletico its football pitch. But, she says, they also "eliminated all the trees in a district already deprived of green spaces to create five paddle courts (…) Whether it is by the bars, the takeaways, the AirBnBs or the padel courts, San Lorenzo is a neighborhood destined to make profit by consumption." Nonetheless, the Atletico, established by San Lorenzo's young residents in 2013, has attracted subscribers — comprising thirty different nationalities — from across the city. Participants are attracted by the "inclusive way of being together," as well as by the opportunity of practicing sport at nominal fees.

On our way to our next stop, Antigone, an LGBT-feminist bookshop, we pass by Lavinia Palma's atelier, "one of the few artisans who has been able to remain," says Gigliola. In a district that encompasses only half a square kilometer, San Lorenzo boasts five independent bookshops. While local shops continue to close down, "the neighborhood's bookshops are fundamental safeguards, they offer important high-standard services," as well as spaces where the community can congregate, she says. Giufà alone has hosted over one thousand three hundred book presentations and debates; the art-house Cinema Tibur is another important safeguard.

"The numerous initiatives as well as the intellectual stimulus of the Libera Repubblica are reason enough to stay here," she explains. "The liveability of a neighborhood is not only about decorum and degradation but also about services, sociality, opportunities for inclusion and cultural exchanges. […] It is determined by the quality of relationships that can be constructed in a public space." Certainly, this morning, there is a village vibe to San Lorenzo, and Gigliola takes pleasure in stopping to talk to those we happen to meet. Still, she says, the district has a "double identity between the morning and the night;" when bars open, crowds of young people overrun the streets and drug-dealers are out in force.

In 2018, San Lorenzo hit the national headlines when a young girl was found dead in a derelict building in the Borghetto dei Lucani (Lucani little town): a ten thousand square meter complex of workshops, shacks and warehouses, many abandoned. Via dei Lucani is our last stop on Gigliola's tour. The Libera Repubblica worked on a participatory design scheme, together with the 5-star party urban counsellor Luca Montuori, and Roma Capitale to revamp the Borghetto as a green oasis with sports facilities, services, and artisans' studios. It also provided a safe public space for young people, she says. The project was approved but the local government fell before they could pass the final vote. Meanwhile, private developers formed a consortium to pursue their own projects which include more luxury housing and garages.

We watch their cranes at work on the new constructions in the Borghetto. Around the corner, at the end of the road, the luxury Student Hotel, furnished with a rooftop pool, is nearly completed. Via dei Lucani is a frontier road. On one side of the Borghetto stands Communia, a former derelict warehouse, occupied and restored by students and activists ten years ago; it vaunts a tailor atelier run by immigrants, a huge library and a unique study-room, managed by Sharewood, a students' association. Alessandro told me that in an area often controlled by drug-dealers, even the police describe Communia as 'an enclave of safety'. And yet, the building has been auctioned to a US private equity firm, and now Communia faces eviction. On the other side of the Borghetto, the artists' collective Ombrelloni (Big Umbrellas), has rehabilitated an ex-umbrella production workshop. It is faced, across the street, by the headquarters/laboratory of the architecture/research collective Stalker.

It has started to rain, and we take shelter at the bookshop café Tomo, packed with students hunched over their computers. After "many disappointments and defeats, […] it is a moment of reflection," says Gigliola. "As the Libera Repubblica redefines ways of being present on the ground, it needs," she adds with unwavering optimism, "to adapt to new realities." Gigiola looks forward to organizing assemblies with the new generation, "the students in their tents," camping in front of the university to protest against Rome's exorbitant rents. To grow as a community and to raise awareness among the young are the priorities, as is reaching out to the new immigrant population. "As regards neighborhood transformations, every neighborhood has a point of no return," she says. Her dream and hope are that "we have not reached the point of no return, that we can still exert influence."

Alessandra Valentinelli
Photo by CFFC Roma, 2023

# Alessandra/Forum Territoriale
# Parco delle Energie – Lago Ex SNIA

As Italians sat at home watching the evening news during the pandemic lockdown, they were charmed by images of ducks appropriating Rome's historic fountains and grass creeping over the untouched cobblestones of its piazzas. It was comforting to watch nature reclaim their capital city. Yet, spontaneous nature, often unobserved, has always co-inhabited with them.

Rome sprawls over one thousand two hundred square kilometers; it is one of Europe's largest capitals but only around a third of its land has been developed and its population — at just under three million — is relatively small. It contains high numbers of protected green zones and arable land as well as levels of biodiversity unmatched by most European cities. For centuries, an indomitable urban wilderness has been recovering territory; conquering the archaeological ruins celebrated by Piranesi, it is now clambering up abandoned construction sites and taking over the capital's numerous residual spaces. As environmental activism gathers momentum world-wide, in Rome, an innovative community-led socio-ecological movement has emerged, shaped — in part — by the peculiarities of the city's urban landscape. The Lago Ex SNIA (Ex SNIA Lake) has become a symbol of this movement: an accidental lake formed by a failed attempt at real estate speculation.

Walking down the deafeningly noisy, six-lane arterial road, Via di Portonaccio, I nearly missed the entrance to the lake: a small opening in a long wall hidden under the railway tracks. It is difficult to imagine that the capital's only natural lake is buried in one of its most densely inhabited districts: Pigneto-Prenestino. And yet, to cross the park's threshold is to stumble into a strange wilderness where the cacophonous sounds of the city soon give way to birdsong. Alessandra Valentinelli, a member the neighborhood organization, the Forum Ex SNIA, is waiting for me. We walk down the path to catch a glimpse of the lake, partially concealed by thickets of black locust trees and white willows intertwined with tangled masses of marsh reeds accessible only to animals. Ducks are splashing in the water by the haunting frame structure of an uncompleted shopping mall that looms in the background, adding allure to this urban sanctuary. Opposite the lake, we observe the ruins of the former textile factory, the SNIA Viscosa, its crumbling tuff walls redeemed by vegetation. The tables and benches are all taken and Alessandra leads me to a seat in the *barca dei pirati* (the pirate's boat), a wooden construction for children, built by activists. She points to the plants scaling the ruin's façade, a nesting refuge for birds, she tells me. "Falcons, herons and kingfishers have been spotted here," she says.

Alessandra was born in Venice and studied architecture at Milan's Polytechnic where, impressed by some of the urbanists she met, she decided to specialize in urbanism, a profession she chose because of its "usefulness to society." In 2005 she moved to Rome with her daughter, taking up residence in Pigneto. Alessandra has always loved Rome; most of all, she "appreciates the civic sense of its citizens." From her first day, she was made to feel at home not only by her neighbors but also by tradesmen; her plumber and her electrician helped her settle in. When, by chance, her next-door neighbor told her about the battle to preserve the district's only green zone, Alessandra immediately joined the local assembly, "hoping that sharing my skills as an urbanist and an environmental consultant would be a way of giving back something to the community; a way of thanking my plumber and electrician," she says laughingly. She has done much more, when necessary, working full time. Between her professional work and a conference on the lake, a public reforestation workshop and a meeting with the local committee, it was hard to find a time to meet. She shrugs off compliments, remarking that "every citizen should take care of their community. [...] To participate is to compensate for the absence of public support in Rome," she tells me. Tall, with a mane of fair hair, Alessandra's firm gaze betrays a steely tenacity that would otherwise be disguised by an unassuming manner and a soft-spoken voice. She calmly recounts the turbulent history of the Lago Ex SNIA.

In the early 1990s, a Roman developer set about converting the SNIA Viscosa — an abandoned textile factory in disuse since 1954 — into Rome's biggest shopping center. Such a big real estate project in this high-density district was opposed by the local community who sought to safeguard the only green area in the district. When builders began excavating a pit for the parking lot, they accidentally hit an aquifer; water flooded the cavity and proved impossible to divert to the sewers. The ten thousand square meter Lago Ex SNIA was formed around the concrete skeleton of the doomed shopping mall. Meanwhile, the Regione Lazio blocked construction rights because of irregularities in the cadastral map.

Since then, this twelve-hectar plot of land has become the epicenter of an ongoing battle between the developer — who has never given up on building, albeit on a shrinking area of land — and local residents who have never lost their determination to protect a natural resource. Over the last thirty years, residents and activists have been joined by environmentalists, academics, artists and even a famous rap band, Assalti Frontali. They have managed to resist numerous attempts at speculation, including plans for a swimming pool for the 2009 world championships, the construction of residential towers, and the demolition of the factory buildings that are now listed industrial archaeological monuments. They have also won some significant victories: in1997, they convinced the local government to expropriate the hill and protected pine forest above the lake to create a seven- hectar public park, the Parco delle Energie;[50] in

---

[50] Next to the Parco delle Energie stands the Centro Sociale CSOA. In 1995, activists occupied a factory building to defend the ecological zone. There, they found thousands of documents on former factory

2008, they established the Forum Territoriale Parco delle Energie — Lago Ex SNIA, a self-managed neighborhood organization that oversees the park and the lake; and in 2014 they rallied thousands of Rome's denizens to persuade Roma Capitale to forge a public entrance to the lake that was inaccessible through the park. Finally, in 2020, the Forum persuaded the Regione Lazio to declare the park and the lake a natural monument. Notwithstanding, the struggle is not over. The developer still owns a quarter of the land by the lake and has announced that he has permission to convert the old factory ruins into a huge logistics hub. Meanwhile, the Forum is campaigning for expropriation of the remaining land.

Listening to the story of this relentless confrontation, I wondered how Alessandra and the Forum maintain their resolve. "Are there ever times when you have had enough?" I ask her. "Never," she replies, "for a while the Forum had a slogan *Non lamentarti, partecipa!* (Don't complain, participate!) That is the key, if there is something you don't like, do something about it, don't expect others to do it for you [...] and don't let things crush you." She is motivated by what she calls the "enriching experience of being part of the Forum:" an assembly of residents from all walks of life; botanists, zoologists, ecologists, architects and activists. All decisions are taken collectively in monthly meetings. "Through this forceful amalgamation of energy and skills, we find solutions we would never have imagined. [...] And,

---

workers (mainly women) that are now part of the fascinating archive, the *Centro di Documentazione Maria Baccante*, in the Casa del Parco.

together it is fun!" she exclaims. It is a constant learning process. Alessandra stresses the importance of raising awareness, particularly among the younger generations. She dedicates much of her time to informing people about the lake and involving schools, the neighborhood — sometimes the whole city — in the Forum's activities. Sabrina Baldacci, a veteran activist at the Forum, describes Alessandra as "a driving force of the Forum."

We walk to pick up her dog at her flat, overrun by plants of all sizes and books squeezed into every available space. The lake was abandoned for decades, she continues, and undisturbed by man; a remarkable ecosystem has evolved, one that nurtures ninety different bird species and supports nine EU priority habitats. Nutrients in the lake's waters nourish over three hundred and fifty different plant types. "It has become a stop-over for birds in migration," she says proudly. Since the Forum started taking care of the lake, specialists monitor progress and advise on conservation. In a heavily built-up area, this urban oasis absorbs carbon dioxide and mitigates pollution and extreme temperatures during the torrid Roman summer. It also helps draw the neighborhood together. Members of the Senegalese community in Pigneto are employed as custodians of this bucolic public park where the placard at the entrance reads 'it is not forbidden to play ball, get dirty, laugh out-loud, jump, run and scream for joy'. Tens of thousands of people have attended a myriad of debates, concerts, performances, and workshops managed or hosted by the Forum. Honey from the onsite apiary helps cover maintenance costs.

But "common goods are always the most fragile element of the city," Alessandra comments, somberly. Pheasants disappeared when the developer recently removed the vegetation around the ruins, "but plants can regrow. It is the potential demolition of the factory ruins and the construction of new buildings near the lake that could cause devastation. If birds can't nest on the ruins, they will leave and the whole ecosystem could collapse." The next battle will be to expropriate the remaining land and return it to the community. Alessandra is unruffled. "It will be interesting — we will see," she says.

"The fight is not only for urban green spaces, it is also about defending eco-system processes and biodiversity," she continues, "it is a vision for the city, not just for the district: a strategy to combat climate change." While EU directives encourage investment in rewilding and increasing biodiversity, in Rome nature has taken its own revenge, spontaneously rewilding an abandoned building site. The lake is an inherent part of an ecological network that one day, the Forum hopes, will extend across the city. To this end, it collaborates with resident committees nearby at the Parco Pubblico di Centocelle, the Villa Certosa, the Pratone di Torre Spaccata, and the Parco Lineare. Most of the territory is part of the old Sistema Direzionale Orientale (SDO): a mishmash of both public and private land; neglected public parks and decaying archaeological monuments; sectors designated for public green zones and then abandoned; unbuilt land belonging to developers and urban wilderness. Rome abounds with local committees: dedicated citizens seeking to protect natural resources. As for the role played by

Roma Capitale,[51] "environmental issues cut across politics," says Alessandra. She sees little difference between left and right-wing administrations although she has praise for Luca Montuori, the 5-Star party Urban Counsellor, with whom there was a dialogue.

There is a struggle ahead but, for now, "we are winning. We can be happy!" exclaims Alessandra. In the words of Assalti Frontali and the Il Muro del Canto in *Il Lago che combatte* [The lake that fights]:

> In mezzo ai mostri de cemento / il lago è 'n sogno che s'avvera: / 'E la natura che resiste / stanotte Roma è meno nera
> [In the midst of concrete monsters / the lake is a dream come true: / It is nature that resists / tonight Rome is less dark.]

---

[51] Rome's Municipal Government

From the left: Stefania Ficacci, Alessandra Broccolini, Romina Peritore, Stefania Favorito, Claudio Gnessi and Carmelo Russo.
Photo by Luisa Fabriziani, 2019

# Stefania/Ecomuseo Casilino

Stefania had a dream the night before we met. She dreamt that she participated in a documentary filmed in an old village where "there were still artisans and everybody was working together; they were showing how things used to be done: making polenta, beating clothes on a stone, building homes." But Stefania could not stop crying. When the director asked her why, she replied, "because all of this no longer exists, and I want this! […] The community, the village where everyone is together," she later told me. Her work at the Ecomuseo Casilino, is directed at "being together."

During the Christmas holidays, we texted arrangements to meet at the Villa De Sanctis park between Centocelle and Tor Pignattara in south-east Rome. "We will end (the walk) in a bar and have a glass of prosecco; this is also what I do!" she exclaimed. I liked her already.

Once again, I take the Metro C and arrive at the Gardenie stop in Centocelle.[52] From there it is a short walk to the Villa de Sanctis, passing by the towering Casilino 23 housing blocks — built in the late 1970s with a masterplan by the architect Ludovico Quaroni. A few seconds later, I catch sight of the majestic Mausoleum of Saint' Elena. A group of Bangladeshi children are playing catch by the entrance to the Villa; families are walking their dogs; a young couple saunter along the lane — hand in hand. It is an unexpected and idyllic setting in the heart of a populated district. Stefania is waiting for me, seated on a bench; elegantly dressed in black with her long blonde hair tied back in a ponytail. We skip formalities and she dives into the story of the Villa de Sanctis. I learn that she is a professional guide as well as an archaeologist. Stefania tells me that while the De Sanctis family donated the Villa and the land to the local government in the 1950s, it was rented and sub-rented for decades, and it was not until 1994 that the local government — under continuous pressure from residents — finally retook possession of the territory to create a public park. "The south-east has always been fiery," she says, "if there is no pressure from below, they (public authorities) don't do anything."

Still, some of the land around the park is in the hands of developers.[53] "We were born to stop them," says Stefania, "and to combat property speculation." Stefania, Alessandra Broccolini, Stefania Ficacci, Claudio Gnessi and Romina

---

[52] One can also take the white and yellow train from Termini to Centocelle, affectionately known as the 'trenino'.
[53] The territory is part of the former SDO, see Pg 68.

Peritore — the five founders of Ecomuseo Casilino — "met by chance," she continues, "when we heard about the attack on the land in 2009 — a development project to build three thousand residential apartments," backed by the then mayor, Gianni Alemanno. They were all local residents and volunteers, "each one with a different skill." Uniting with the neighborhood committees, they "began to write, organize meetings (and protests) and get to know each other." They also launched a robust social media campaign. Eventually, they thwarted the project, and in 2012 the group set up the association Ecomuseo Casilino Ad Duas Lauros. Stefania gestures towards an abandoned field in the distance, "every time they try and build there, we block the development," she says, smiling. Sometimes they fail. Stefania points to the other side of park on the Via Casilina, "see where they are constructing now, its public land up to the fencing; when you cross it, it becomes a monster," she says. Stefania speaks passionately about her work at the Ecomuseo; yet she is also a counsellor as well as a volunteer for other Roman grassroots organizations, managing to juggle those commitments with full-time work and the raising of two sons. Besides possessing indefatigable energy — I wonder out loud — she must be an optimist. "I am a fighter," she replies swiftly.

As an open-air museum, the Ecomuseo Casilino has no headquarters. Instead, it oversees a segment of a huge archaeological zone called the Comprensorio Ad Duas Lauros;[54] primarily, the area from Porta Maggiore (the eastern gate in the Aurelian walls) to Centocelle, and from

---

[54] Subject to the archaeological constraint Ad Duas Lauros.

the Centocelle Archaeological Park to the Villa Gordiani: the 'green lungs' of east Rome. The concept of an Ecomuseum was developed in France in the early 1970s, by Georges Henri Rivière and Hugues de Varine. Unlike traditional museums that concentrate on specific items and objects, an ecomuseum takes an anthropological approach. It advances cultural heritage — both the tangible and intangible — focusing on cultural identity shaped by physical space: buildings, landscape, and urban landscape — and the memories they evoke — and by local traditions, beliefs, and customs. Oral histories can play an important role.

We walk to the Mausoleum; the entrance is hidden off the Via Casilina. Stefania has bought innumerable visitors to the site and yet her eyes still gleam with the eagerness of someone on their first visit. The building, she explains, is part of the Ad Duas Lauros (the Two Laurels), an ancient Roman complex of buildings that include both the Villa 'Ad Duas Lauros' and two other Roman villas in the Centocelle Park. The Mausoleum was built to house the Emperor Costantine's tomb but was later assigned to his mother Elena in 330 A.D. Stefania proudly shows me the amphorae[55] that were used to lighten the weight of the dome. The edifice is also known as Tor Pignattara (the Tower of the Amphorae) from which derives the toponym for the local neighborhood. Nearby stand the magnificently frescoed fourth-century catacombs of Marcellinus and Peter. "Nonetheless," exclaims Stefania, "many Romans are unaware of their existence." Tourists rarely venture here.

---

[55] Pignatte is the Italian word for Roman amphorae.

"Look at the beautiful view!" exclaims Stefania as we turn the corner. I am also taken aback by the grandeur of the third-century Acquedotto Alessandrino amid these dense urban surroundings. "It extends for twenty-two kilometers!" says Stefania. She guides me to the Madonna della Capannuccia (Madonna of the Tiny Hut.) It is said that in the late 1940s, children from the near-by shacks[56] fled in fear when they were confronted with the vision of the Madonna, taking refuge in a hut that was later transformed into this miniscule chapel, self-managed by the community. Every inch of the wall space is taken over by ex votos, interspersed with figurines, and photographs of saints. Further down the road, past a huge mural with portraits of local heroes,[57] lies the Parco Giordano Sangalli: a long stretch of land that flanks the aqueduct.[58] "It was frequented by drug-pushers," explains Stefania; "a no man's land with tons of garbage," she adds. Then neighborhood committees, supported by the Ecomuseo, started to take care of the park themselves, organizing events to encourage residents to frequent an area that they had avoided for years. While the park is now supported by the local municipality, the Comitato Spontaneo Aquedotto Alessandrino (the Spontaneous

---

[56] During and after WWII, makeshift homes and shacks were constructed in the arches of the aqueducts by those made homeless as well as immigrants, mainly from southern Italy.

[57] Street art murals abound in Tor Pignattara; some have been commissioned by the local community in collaboration with the Ecomuseo.

[58] Named after the local partisan, Giordano Sangalli. These are neighborhoods known for their resistance to the fascist regime and later to the Nazi occupation.

Committee of Aqueduct Alessandrino) continues to take charge of its preservation.

Scenes from the popular Italian film 'Bangla'[59] were shot in the vicinity. The film draws from the director Phaim Bhuiyan's own experience as a second-generation Italian, of Bangladeshi origin, born in Tor Pignattara. Tor Pignattara's "Bangladeshi community is the largest in Europe," says Stefania, as we stroll down Via di Tor Pignattara. And there is always something familiar about this noisy bustling neighborhood defined by its long narrow streets and animated by blazing colors and spicy smells that are redolent of London's East End many years ago. I could be in any northern European metropolis were it not for the decidedly Mediterranean vibe. A vino e olio (wine and oil shop), a halal butcher, a kebab take-away, a Chinese grocery all share the same sidewalk, as do an Indian restaurant and a Bangladeshi barber, in close proximity to the Pasticceria Signorini, one of Rome's oldest cake shops. Claudio Gnessi, the president of the Ecomuseo, whom I spoke to earlier, describes the district as the "Rome that is coming, or the Italy that is coming."

We continue our conversation over an abundant midday aperitivo at Stefania's bar, followed by a delicious meal in an Afghani canteen, one of Stefania's favorite haunts. "Why did the Bangladeshi community choose this neighborhood?" I ask her. "Because their concept of a house resembles these houses," she replies, pointing to the two and three-story buildings

---

[59] *Bangla* is a film released in 2019, written and directed by Phaim Bhuiyan who also plays the main role.

through the window. "There is a human dimension here [...] and the houses were cheap to rent in the 1980 and 1990s, when they started arriving." Extended families soon began to cram into small apartments. The history of the neighborhood during the twentieth century is one of immigration: first, builders and workers from the south, later, the Bangladeshi en masse and the Chinese. There are tensions at times. There are those Italians who had lived here for generations who feel that foreigners have usurped the district's identity; they "defend their Italianicity," says Stefania. Some have moved out. Cultural integration is stronger among the young. The Scuola Pisacane, the local school, successfully caters for the needs of children and teenagers of eighteen different nationalities.

The organization has two missions, she clarifies: to defend and revalorize the territory, and to develop a 'collective identity' shaped both by tangible and intangible culture. "The Ecomuseo is what we are doing now," says Stefania, smiling; it is a shorter itinerary. By collaborating with residents on 'community mapping' to single out landmarks of particular significance, the museum has identified historical and archaeological circuits, green paths, spiritual paths, Italian cinema routes,[60] and many more guided walks open to the general public. Stefania recounts bringing kids from Casilino 23 to visit the Saint'Elena mausoleum. "Wow! they say; they are astounded," she comments; as are children from the Bangladeshi community. This may be a poorer neighborhood now but it was once the home of Rome's

---

[60] Some famous Italian Neorealist films were shot here.

Emperors, she reminds me. In the film Bangla, Phaim introduces himself as "50% Italiano, 50% Bangla e 100% di Tor Pigna" (I am 50% Italian, 50% Bangladeshi and 100% from Tor Pigna').[61] "The more you stick to history, the better you defend yourself," she continues. Working alongside local committees, the Ecomuseo has helped to destigmatize what "used to be considered a ghetto neighborhood," she says, and promote a shared sense of place.

Collaborating with local schools is a priority. Claudio estimates that they run around fifty to sixty workshop programs every year, aimed at children from nursery school age to young people in their late teens. Workshops are also conducted in the local mosques. Laboratories on local historical and artistic heritage alternate with workshops on religious festivals (of all religions) and on the cultural traditions of the diverse ethnic groups that inhabit the neighborhood. The museum's work has not gone unnoticed. In 2019, it was acknowledged by the Lazio Region's authorities as an Ecomuseum of regional importance, and in 2023 it was accredited by UNESCO as an NGO that safeguards intangible cultural heritage.

"L'Ecomuseo is like crochet [...] working on little things but slowly crocheting a huge jersey," says Stefania. There have been numerous battles; their victories, she explains, owe much to community cohesion. "If we don't understand that alone, we suffer, and together, we can feel good, then we have not understood anything [...] being together is fundamental and it is something we are losing!" she exclaims.

---

[61] Diminutive of Tor Pignattara.

# Acknowledgements

My research is indebted to: Carlo Cellamare and LabSU, the multi-disciplinary Urban Studies Laboratory that he directs at La Sapienza University; Stalker/Osservatorio Nomade, an architecture/research/activist collective that explored many of the themes discussed in this book some thirty years ago; and Giorgio de Finis and his pioneering work at the MAAM and the Museo delle Periferie.

I am also grateful to my family and to friends — old and new — who have patiently made suggestions — and corrections: Ginevra Bompiani, Sara Braschi, Paola Cantini, Francesco Careri, Maria Claudia Clemente, Sarah Linford, Francesco Montillo, Luca Montuori, Cesare Pietroiusti, Sofia Sebastianelli, and Philip Watson; and especially to Ludovico Pratesi, Jeffrey Kennedy, and Gaia, Zoe, and Andrea Carlino.

I thank Francesco Careri for his beautiful Preface.

Finally, a sincere thanks to: Quarticciolo Ribelle, Fondazione Piccolo America, Scomodo, Donnexstrada, Cubo Libro, Angelo Mai Altrove, Post Ex, Calciosociale, Termini tv and Mama Termini, Libera Repubblica di San Lorenzo, Forum Parco delle Energie — Lago Ex SNIA, and the Ecomuseo Casilino.

Articles on some of these organizations have been published in journals that include: ArchDaily, JoCA, RIBA journal, the Developer and, in particular, Common Edge.

# Appendix

## Recommendations

Each organization recommends places to visit and/or their favorite bars:

### Quarticciolo Ribelle
**IG:** instagram.com/quarticcioloribelle
**IG:** instagram.com/palestrapopolarequarticciolo
**FB:** facebook.com/quarticciolo.ribelle

We recommend:
Il Bar di Rosi — via Castellaneta (Teatro Biblioteca Quarticciolo).
L'VIII lotto — via Ostuni (one of the neighborhood's most beautiful housing units).
La Casa di Quartiere — via Trani, 1.
Il Parchetto Modesto di Veglia — via Ugento, 30 (opened thanks to Quarticciolo Ribelle and la Comunità Educante della Borgata).
L'Ex Questura — piazza del Quarticciolo (a squat with an after-school laboratory and a brewery — and with accommodation on the top floors).

## Fondazione Piccolo America
**Website Cinema Troisi:** cinematroisi.it
**Website Piccolo America:** piccoloamerica.it
**FB Cinema Troisi:** facebook.com/CinemaTroisi
**FB Piccolo America:** facebook.com/piccoloamerica
**IG Cinema Troisi:** instagram.com/cinematroisi
**IG Piccolo America:** instagram.com/piccoloamerica

We recommend:
(Bars and food shops)
Augustarello — vicolo De Renzi, 15.
Bar San Calisto — piazza di San Calisto, 3.
Norcineria Iacozzilli — via Natale del Grande, 15.
Venanzio (Supplì) — via di S. Francesco a Ripa, 137.
Adrian's casa del gelato — viale Ettore Franceschini, 75 (Colli Aniene).

## Scomodo

**Website:** scomodo.org
**Redazione IG:** instagram.com/laredazioneroma
**Redazione FB:** facebook.com/LaRedazioneScomodo
**Scomodo IG:** instagram.com/leggiscomodo
**Scomodo FB:** facebook.com/LeggiScomodo

We recommend:
Cinema Troisi — via Girolamo Induno, 1.
Spin Time and all the places inside it: a world to discover — via di S. Croce in Gerusalemme, 55.
Ala 34, a coworking space — via di Affogalasino, 34.
Angelo Mai Altrove — viale delle Terme di Caracalla, 55.
Fanfulla — via Fanfulla da Lodi, 5a (music).
Trenta Formiche — via del Mandrione, 3 (music).
Piazza Gianicolo: Scomodo's summer space in Rome.

## Donnexstrada
**Website:** donnexstrada.org
**IG:** instagram.com/donnexstrada
**FB:** facebook.com/Donnexstrada
**LinkedIn:** linkedin.com/company/donnexstrada

We recommend:
Lucha Y Siesta — via Lucio Sestio, 10.
Cinema Troisi (punto viola) — via Girolamo Induno, 1.
La Redazione Scomodo, Spintime — via di S. Croce in Gerusalemme, 55.
Angelo Mai Altrove — viale delle Terme di Caracalla, 55.
Enoteca Il Piccolo — via del Governo Vecchio, 74-75: where we signed our covenant.

## Cubo Libro
**Website:** cubolibro.org
**FB:** facebook.com/CuboLibro
**IG:** instagram.com/cubolibro

We recommend:
Website: torbellamonaca.com
Il Teatro di Tor Bella Monaca — via Bruno Cirino, 5 (theater).
La Pizzetta — via Acquaroni, 106.
Io e Walter (pizzeria) in the Le Torri shopping mall — via Michele Buonori, 19.
Ciclofficina La Gabbia — largo Ferruccio Mengaroni, 11 (bicycle repair shop).
Aula Vicina Piano Terra — viale Duilio Cambellotti, 167 B (family center for children 0-3 years).

## Angelo Mai Altove
**Website:** angelomai.org
**FB:** facebook.com/angelomai
**IG:** instagram.com/angelo_mai_roma

We recommend:
Teatro Valle Occupato — via del Teatro Valle, 21.
Libreria/ Bar Tuba — via del Pigneto, 39/a. (a women's bookshop).
Spin Time — via di S. Croce in Gerusalemme, 55.
Angelo Mai a Monti — via degli Zingari.

## Post Ex
**IG:** instagram.com/post_ex_post_ex

We recommend: (Artist-run spaces)
Spazio Insitu: spazioinsitu.it
Spazio Mensa: instagram.com/spaziomensa
Condotto 48: condotto48.com
Paese Fortuna: instagram.com/paesefortuna
Porto Simpatica: instagram.com/portosimpatica

## Calciosociale
**Website:** calciosociale.it
**FB**: facebook.com/calciosocialeitalia
**IG**: instagram.com/calciosociale

We recommend:
The House of Spirituality next to the Campo dei Miracoli.
The parking lot — via Mazzacurati, a former rubbish dump that the Calciosociale team converted into a parking lot.
The Fratelli Cervi School (the local school) — via Mazzacurati, 90.
The Farmers Market — via Mazzacurati, 75.

## Termini tv/Mama Termini

**FB:** facebook.com/terminitv and facebook.com/mamatermini
**IG:** instagram.com/terminitv and instagram.com/mamatermini

We recommend:
The Acquario Romano and its garden — piazza Manfredo Fanti.
The area behind via Volturno — with its Filipino, Ethiopian and Peruvian restaurants.
The Roman walls that lead towards San Lorenzo.
The gallery above the regional train's railway lines: a poetical place.
The Servian Wall at Termini and its remains both inside and outside the station.

## Libera Repubblica di San Lorenzo
**Website:** liberarepubblicadisanlorenzo.info/wp
**FB:** facebook.com/LiberaRepubblicaDiSanLo

We recommend:
Ex Cinema Palazzo — piazza dei Sanniti.
The bookshops: Giufà Libreria Caffè — via degli Aurunci, 38; Tomo Libreria Caffé — via degli Etruschi, 4; Libreria Antigone — via dei Piceni, 1.
Communia — viale dello Scalo San Lorenzo, 33.
Parco dei Caduti — piazza dei Caduti (park).
The book: Dopo la gentrificazione: Un quartiere laboratorio dalla crisi economica all'abitare temporaneo, by Alessandro Barile, Barbara Brollo, Sarah Gainsforth, Rosella Marchini, DeriveApprodi, 2023.

## Forum Territoriale Parco delle Energie – Lago Ex SNIA

**Website:** lagoexsnia.wordpress.com/author/exsnia
**FB:** facebook.com/lagoexsnia
**IG:** instagram.com/lagobullicante.exsnia

We recommend:
Il Quadrato — Parco delle Energie — via Prenestina, 175 : a multi-purpose space in the Parco delle Energie.
CSOA Ex Snia — via Prenestina,173.
Bookshop bar Tuba — via del Pigneto, 39/a.
Bookshop café Lo Yeti — via Perugia, 4.

## Ecomuseo Casilino
**Website:** ecomuseocasilino.it
**FB:** facebook.com/ecomuseocasilino
**IG:** instagram.com/ecomuseocasilino

We recommend:
The underground Basilica of Porta Maggiore — via Prenestina, 17.
MAUMi: Museo di Arte Urbana sulla Migrazioni — via Casilina, 634 (Urban Art Museum on Migration), maumimuseum.com
Fortezza Est — via Francesco Laparelli, 62 (bookshop).
Bazar Taverna Curdo Meticcia — via Casilina, 607.
Santa Libberata/La Carretteria — via Galeazzo Alessi, 96.

www.ingramcontent.com/pod-product-compliance
Lightning Source LLC
Chambersburg PA
CBHW071711020426
42333CB00017B/2224